31
242

PROFESSIONAL COUNSELING ON HUMAN BEHAVIOR:

Its Principles and Practices

PROFESSIONAL COUNSELING ON HUMAN BEHAVIOR:

Its Principles and Practices

by Douglass W. Orr, M.D.

FORMER DIRECTOR,
SEATTLE PSYCHOANALYTIC INSTITUTE

FRANKLIN WATTS, INC.
575 Lexington Avenue, New York, N.Y. 10022

FIRST PRINTING
© Copyright 1965 by Douglass W. Orr
Library of Congress Catalog Card Number: 65-13682
Printed in the United States of America

Contents

Preface

The term *counseling* has connotations that range from offering advice about the choice of a career to recommending treatment by a psychoanalyst. Counseling can be a kind of teaching (imparting facts), advising (making suggestions), or therapy (helping with emotional problems or problems of social functioning). It can, of course, be combinations of these and other ways of helping people.

The variety of counselors is equally diverse. People with personal problems turn to clergymen, physicians, psychologists, marriage counselors, social workers, lawyers, teachers, and others. Over 70 per cent will go initially to clergymen or family doctors; i.e., physicians other than psychiatrists. Only about 25 per cent will consult initially those who have been the most thoroughly trained for counseling: social workers, psychiatrists, and clinical psychologists. These ironic facts are among the findings of the Joint Commission on Mental Illness and Health.[1] (References appear at the end of the Preface and at the end of each chapter. A list of books for further reading may be found at the end of the book.)

We shall not be concerned here with questions of who

should be counselors. We wish, rather, to be helpful to those who are. The fact is that clergymen and doctors have been counselors for generations. Social workers, psychiatrists, and their kind are relative newcomers. It is only in recent years that counseling has become so highly skilled. Modern insights into human personality have better defined the problems of counseling and refined its techniques. An equally important fact is that clergymen and physicians are increasingly better trained for counseling. Much of their teaching and supervision is at the hands of social workers, psychiatrists, and psychologists, just as in former years social workers used psychiatrists—particularly psychoanalysts —as their principal teachers and consultants.

Those who teach also learn, and those who learn teach. Cross-fertilization is the order of the day among the helping professions. It is for this reason that we can address ourselves to all groups that engage in counseling. Granting differences in training, in skills, and in the diversity of professional lives apart from counseling, everyone who counsels has very much in common. The clients of all groups are more similar than unique, and their problems are those of human beings everywhere. The basic knowledge of human personality is the same for all and the applications of this knowledge become less distinctive with each passing year.

This book will be devoted principally to counseling as therapy. That is, we shall be concerned with counseling of people whose problems go beyond the need for facts or direct advice. We shall not, therefore, discuss educational or vocational guidance or, for example, the purely factual aspects of premarital counseling or planned parenthood. In this context these are predominantly educational rather than counseling procedures.

We shall be very much concerned, however, with questions of what to do about the person who comes for facts or guidance about specific matters, but who, in doing so, reveals deeper and more pervasive problems. The difficulties of a given client are not always indicated by the initial formulation of his request or by the specialty of the person to whom he comes initially. The question: "May I join the Peace Corps?" can hide a deeper question: "Am I able to leave my parents' home?" The first question calls for evaluation and decision; the second, for counseling or other therapy.

It may be odd and even presumptuous for a psychoanalyst to write about counseling. I cheerfully concede both possibilities. I am, however, a physician with *some* experience of general practice both during the Depression and in the Navy. I have been colleague and consultant to teachers, psychologists, social workers, and psychiatrists in a variety of agency, clinic, and other treatment settings from the Southard School of the Menninger Clinic in Topeka, Kansas (1938) to the Family Counseling Service of Seattle, Washington (1964). I have become familiar with counseling activities of clergymen and physicians, and my analytic patients have included representatives of virtually all helping professions. During the past several years, my wife has resumed her social work education, and discussions with her have been an important stimulus to the writing of this book. For the sake of her professional reputation, I hasten to add, however, that she is otherwise in no way responsible for the result.

It would take a rare book to satisfy every "school" of counseling. This one certainly will not. As a psychoanalyst, psychotherapist, and consultant to counselors, I have a diagnostic orientation. I fully understand the limitations and even dangers of early diagnosis, especially when its terminology becomes epithet or epitaph. At the same time, however, I believe that preliminary diagnostic evaluation is essential, if only to ensure that medical possibilities are carefully considered and that the client is in the right place for the services that are pertinent and appropriate to his needs.

The following pages reflect inevitably the perspective of a consultant. I have heard much more about problem cases than about successes. Clients discussed with me are frequently those presenting unusual difficulties in diagnosis. At best, therefore, I tend to get a one-sided view of counseling in other than psychiatric settings. Certainly, too, I am limited in my knowledge of professional theory, methods, and practice of counselors in professions other than my own. It is quite possible, therefore, that what I write will satisfy no group of counselors entirely. The contribution I can make, however, derives from a wealth of clinical material and from many discussions with many counselors about the difficulties they have encountered both in diagnosis and in treatment.

This is not a book on theory, and I shall state my theoretical position briefly: There are many professions, but there is only one science of human behavior. That science comprises everything that we know currently about human behavior. It is not limited to one profession or to one department in a university. It is rather the sum total of the behavioral sciences as they are relevant to understanding and working with people who need professional help. This relevance may well be more for diagnosis than for treatment, but even that relevance is of the highest importance.

It is essential, I think, to distinguish sharply between basic theory and differential practice. I do not believe that theory, in any profession, can be derived exclusively from practice. Practice crystallizes theory and often ossifies it.

Theory of human behavior is generic, but how it is applied depends upon a myriad of variables affecting the counselor, the professional setting, the client, and the client's problems.

I do not suggest that all counselors should be trained alike. A basic knowledge of human behavior is certainly a common denominator of all the helping professions, but this is not where education stops. The future counselor should know everything possible about the psycho-socio-biological nature of man, but after that he will, depending upon his chosen field, learn specialized facts about pneumonia, or community organization, or psychological testing, or a host of other matters. He will also learn the scope and methods of his profession in whatever field or setting he intends to work; that is, a differential application of his basic training.

When a counselor sees a client, he needs to know enough to make—or to insist upon getting—a psycho-socio-biological diagnosis, but what he does about this, once the diagnosis is at least suspected, is a matter of his skills and limitations, of his preferences and aversions, of the authority invested in him by law, or the demands of professional tradition, and of whether he practices his profession in private office, hospital, clinic, church, social agency, school, or client's home. In my opinion, no discipline can afford to focus upon the part-individual until safeguarded by a working diagnosis of the whole. When this is before us we can enjoy the luxury of specialization!

This book does not repeat the theoretical content of any profession. It takes for granted aspects of such knowledge that apply to all. It aims to be practical in bridging the gap between generic theory and its direct application in a variety of situations and with a multiplicity of clients. It deals with problems of counselors as well as of clients in order that other counselors may anticipate such difficulties and avoid them.

Let me state again that I write from a consultant's point of view. If I pick up the "blind spots" and mistakes of others, it is because this is what I have been paid to do. It does not imply that I have no blind spots and make no mistakes. One can almost always be more discerning and objective about another's work than about his own.

In what follows, everyone is a counselor or a client. If true identities were revealed, some clients would be patients; and some counselors would be social workers, speech therapists, clergymen, psychologists, and physicians. By the same token, both counselors and clients will generally be referred to as "he" or "him." It is usually simpler this way, but I shall not permit a foolish consistency to dictate the writing of every line.

I would like to express my gratitude to my wife, Jean Walker Orr. It is nearly thirty years since we collaborated on a book, the earlier one describing the pre-World War II compulsory health insurance scheme in Britain. Her responsibility here is limited, however; I am accountable for all shortcomings of commission or omission.

Helen Harris Perlman asked skeptical questions and made helpful suggestions when I set out to write this book. She may disavow the use to which I put these suggestions, but I appreciate them nonetheless. I am grateful, too, to the Family Counseling Service of Seattle for a happy and rewarding association—intermittent though it has been—since 1941. My debt to the Menninger Foundation is very great, not only because of my training there, but also because of related teaching and consultation assignments at three universities, a public clinic, and a family counseling agency. I have also learned from psychologists and social workers in a variety of community agencies in Seattle, and from a decade and a half of curious and often challenging medical students and graduate students of social work at the University of Washington.

All case vignettes in this book have, of course, been disguised in order to preclude identification.

When I was very young, I prayed for humility. Since I have had patients in psychoanalysis this has been quite unnecessary. They have eagerly, though unknowingly, helped me to avoid the unexamined life. I shall be greatly disappointed if their efforts are not reflected in these pages!

DOUGLASS W. ORR, M.D.
Seattle, Washington

1. Gerald Gurin, Joseph Veroff, and Sheila Feld, *Americans View Their Mental Health.* Joint Commission on Mental Illness and Health. Monograph Series, No. 4 (New York: Basic Books, Inc., 1960).

Part I

COUNSELORS
AND CLIENTS

CHAPTER ONE

Counseling in Different Settings

Counseling cannot be precisely defined. It is not a single activity nor is it the province of any one profession. The usual dictionary definitions, having to do with giving advice, are too narrow in scope. Today's counselor may give a good deal of advice, or he may give none. Everything depends upon the training and experience of the counselor and the setting in which he works, as well as upon the personality makeup of the client and the nature of his problem.

The breadth and diversity of counseling may be suggested by such characterizations as the following: It is the *art* of helping people to help themselves. It is the applied *science* of psycho-socio-biological pathology. It is the *process* of solving human problems in a professional setting. It is a *relationship* between a trained helping-person and other persons with problems from which the latter draw strength, confidence, and insight in the process of working out their own solutions to their difficulties.

Counseling may, of course, be all of these. It has less the

implication of "to counsel" and more of "to take counsel with," but even this does scant justice to its infinite variety. Let us, therefore, have a look at how opportunities for counseling arise in quite different settings.

A. *Counseling and Consultation*

Mr. Smith consults his lawyer about a will. He gives instructions which the attorney translates into legal form. The focus of this consultation is limited to drawing up the will and subsequently signing it in the presence of witnesses.

Suppose, however, that Smith is a widower, estranged from his children and determined to leave everything to the housekeeper who looks after him. At this point the lawyer is likely to become a counselor. He will tactfully challenge Smith's intentions. He will listen to a recital of grievances about the children. He will ask Smith to clarify all aspects of the situation. He will, in short, do everything he can to .nake certain that what Smith says he intends to do is what he *really* wants to do. In the end he will follow Smith's instructions or refuse to continue as his lawyer, but meanwhile he will have been a counselor.

This is even more the case when an angry Mrs. Jones comes storming in, demanding a divorce from her husband. The typical attorney will quietly resist impulsive actions of this type. He will hear the client out, of course, but will also challenge her intentions, point up the difficulties, delay definitive actions and, in various ways, compel the client to pause, take stock of her feelings, clarify her thinking and, perhaps, in the end, reconsider.

These are not the precise techniques of counseling in all other situations, but they are comparable; and the objectives are the same. Even though the initial focus may be upon a single problem—how to get a divorce—it is skillfully shifted to a total involvement in the client's self-appraisal and comprehensive evaluation of assets and liabilities of the marriage. This course of events might be substantially the same if the client came first to a family doctor, to a clergyman, or to a marriage counselor. This does not mean that the training, experience, skills, or techniques are uniformly similar, but rather that the concerns and goals for the client are very much the same. As to the outcome, who knows how similar or different the therapeutic results may be?

B. *The Doctor's Office*

Consultations with physicians can be equally simple, and equally complex. Mrs. Johnson takes five-year-old Billy to the doctor, and the doctor says: "His tonsils must come out." So, it is a tonsillectomy at age five, or another three, four, or five years of colds, sore throats, earaches, and general sickliness. Mrs. Johnson has her doubts, however, because she knows that surgery at age five (or any age, for that matter) can be felt as punishment, rejection, and abandonment. The doctor tries to reassure her, pointing out at the same time the emotional complications of feeling weak, sick, inferior, and unable to keep up with others. At this point Billy asks in all innocence: "And will the doctor cut off my penie, too?" How rapidly the problem shifts from Billy's tonsils to Billy's apprehensive mother and then to Billy as a whole person with a vivid fantasy life. The doctor becomes a counselor perforce or else he had better ask for help!

Nor is Billy an isolated case. Doctors must, or could, be counselors many times a day. This ulcer or bowel trouble or skin condition is psychosomatic. What are the emotional components and what can be done about them? How to tell the Petersons that their child has a malignant blood condition? The dying patient? The childless couple? The unmarried mother? They all need so much time, but there are "so many things to do and so little time in which to do them."

Most doctors know when a patient wants to talk things over. It is obvious that the patient is bursting with something or, by contrast, that he is strangely quiet. The receptive doctor will ask, "Well, what is it?" or offer "A penny for your thoughts." If this does not occur, the patient will summon up his courage and introduce the subject with "By the way, Doctor . . ." or "I hate to bother you with this, but . . ." or something of the sort. He may be casual and seemingly unconcerned: "I know it's really nothing, but I've noticed a little soreness . . ." *She* may be direct and abrupt: "Why can't I get pregnant?" The doctor should not be deceived. These patients are emotionally upset about something; they want to talk and they need more than peremptory replies.

Doctors should not ignore or brush off such appeals, but the fact is that many do. Some are obtuse because they are unconsciously made anxious by the anxiety of the patient. Others organize their practice to see three, four, or six patients an hour, and will not deviate. Many are inevitably conscious of a waiting room full of other patients, and will, therefore, give quick, commonsense replies, make light of the matter, or somehow dismiss it as quickly as they can. Frequently they leave the patient feeling that they just cannot be bothered.

A host of doctors, fortunately, have quite a different point of view. Their more recent medical school training or special postgraduate courses have made them more aware, more knowledgeable, and more interested. Sensing a counseling problem, they listen to the patient. If necessary, they schedule a second appointment when they will not be rushed. They undertake the counseling job themselves or see to it that the patient gets to someone else after unhurried and carefully considered referral. It takes time and good rapport to get to the problems behind the urgently casual questions. Doctors know this nowadays and are increasingly eager to accept the responsibility for the counseling that is required.

Doctors, overly trained in laboratory science, have been slow to learn the paralyzing effects of anxiety and superstitious fantasy. Even the physician who takes the time to explain things to a patient may forget that the frightened patient cannot really hear his words or distorts them according to his emotional state. Complicating factors, too, are the layman's ignorance of technical vocabularies and the fact that even ordinary words have different meanings for different people.

This kind of jumping to conclusions happens every day:

A patient silently assumed, after surgery for a tubal pregnancy, that she could never again get pregnant. Her depressed feelings complicated, and perhaps induced, a stormy postoperative course. Her doctor finally learned the reason for her emotional upset, brought an anatomy book to her bed, and gave her a detailed explanation of the nature of the Fallopian tubes, the fact that only one had been removed, and the vital fact that her chances of becoming pregnant again were excellent. The patient's concept of herself as a woman was at stake, and the doctor's counseling had both immediate and long-range benefits for her.

Therefore, even if patients have no "extraneous" personal problems to talk about, their routine medical and surgical conditions are often felt as such. Doctors are better informed than formerly about the personal and subjective as well as the social implications of sickness. They know that many patients need counseling, and that this involves careful explanations, time to absorb and work through feelings about what they are told, and further time to wisely make whatever plans the sickness, the operation, or the postoperative situation may require.

Consultation may just as readily reveal the need for counseling with dentists, trust officers, professors, labor leaders, foremen, executives, and countless others. The presenting problem usually calls for direct, uncomplicated answers. Frequently, however, more complex issues are at stake. Worries are revealed, as well as misconceptions, family problems, irrational fears, accident proneness, and indications of a need to fail. The initial question cannot always remain the focal one, but can be dealt with properly only in a larger context; i.e., the context of the whole person who is asking it and of the total environment from which he comes. So it is that consultation leads to counseling or, at least, revelation of the need for it.

C. *Counseling and Guidance*

Guidance has almost as many connotations as *counseling*. Vocational guidance, for example, is usually limited to giving information and advice (frequently based, in part, upon the results of aptitude tests) about the choice of occupation or profession. The guidance department of a public school system, by contrast, enters into problems of adaptation at school—ranging from speech and hearing problems to those of mental retardation and psychiatric illness. A child guidance clinic, again, is generally a psychiatric clinic. *Guidance* may, therefore, have the implication of counseling or other treatment, or it may suggest mainly advisory, liaison, and referral services.

It follows, then, that guidance and counseling may be synonymous. Both may be as limited as imparting facts or as extensive as psychiatric treatment. As in the practice of medicine or law, an initial, limited request can pave the way to more comprehensive treatment. The young man who inquires about the Peace Corps reveals that he left three colleges and four jobs after short periods of time and is urgently in need of extensive counseling. The dull, listless, daydreaming child in third grade may be retarded or worried or simply bored because he is intellectually precocious. The girl applying to enter a convent may have found her vocation, but she may, on the contrary, be seeking an escape from emotional problems that convent life would only accentuate—all of which a "screening committee" would be quite likely to detect, with subsequent referral for some other kind of help.

D. *Counseling and Social Casework*

Counseling and *casework* are just as interchangeable as *counseling* and *guidance*. All social workers study casework and most of them graduate to become counselors in one setting or another. Casework agencies are now commonly known as counseling agencies. Sometimes it seems that one studies casework in order to practice counseling!

Schools of social work differ, of course, but many teach "generic casework." They teach the theoretical background and fundamental principles of the art and science of helping people with their problems, recognizing that the application of this knowledge will vary in practice depending upon the situation in which the individual social worker is employed. Casework is defined by Helen Harris Perlman as a "problem-solving process." The specific application of the knowledge and skills of casework is determined not only by the training and experience of the caseworker, but also by the needs and problems of the client who comes for help, as well as the purposes and resources of the agency that brings worker and client together.

A caseworker in an adoption agency, for example, has a more limited function than one in private practice. His task is to find the best possible home for infants and children who are available for adoption. It is not necessarily part of the agency's function to give casework service to a couple who are refused a child. Prospective adoptive parents frequently, if not routinely, need help with their feelings about such a rejection or with the problem in the home that led to the refusal. Their application may be tabled with a minimum of explanation, however, or they may be referred to a family agency or elsewhere for the counseling they require. Adoption agencies, in other words, sometimes decide that they cannot also be family counseling agencies, and limit themselves accordingly.

Social workers who have had intensive casework training and experience are to be found under various names and in a wide assortment of settings. They may be called medical social workers, psychiatric social workers, family counselors, guidance workers, group workers, or social workers in private practice. Their agency connections may be such that they work primarily with the aged, the physically sick or handicapped, the mentally retarded, unmarried mothers, psychiatric clinic patients, prospective parents, families with marital or other problems, and so on. The scope of their application of casework knowledge and skills can vary as much as that of physicians who range, for example, from country doctors to Mayo Clinic specialists in neurosurgery.

Is it useful to distinguish casework from counseling? Social workers themselves differ as to the connotations of *casework*. It runs the gamut from providing financial assistance to psychotherapy. So, we must add, does counseling. Also, of course, the skillful provision of financial aid is psychotherapeutic, and therefore an aspect of casework or counseling. The sometimes long and intensive effort to help another person with crippling emotional problems (often as not, involving a knowledge of unconscious processes) is likewise a facet of casework or counseling. Another might be to provide homemaker services during the sickness of a mother with small children. There are many techniques for solving human problems, and both caseworkers and counselors (whether with the same or comparable training) are prepared to offer these singly or in combination. Therefore, if it is possible to distinguish counselors from caseworkers, it will be on the basis of details of training, professional affiliation, agency function, or chosen specialization in private practice.

E. *Pastoral Counseling*

According to the report of the Joint Commission on Mental Illness and Health mentioned in the Preface, people turn to clergymen with their personal problems more readily than to any other group. The figures are most interesting: clergymen, 42 per cent; physicians (except psychiatrists), 29 per cent; psychiatrists and psychologists, 18 per cent; social workers and marriage counselors, 16 per cent; lawyers, 6 per cent; others, 11 per cent. The fact that the total exceeds 100 per cent indicates multiple contacts and referrals. The demands upon clergymen explain why pastoral counseling has developed so far and so rapidly in recent years.

Pastoral counseling means, simply, counseling by clergymen. The individual pastoral counselor may or may not have had formal psychiatric, social work, or psychological training in addition to his theological education. He may be a clergyman who has had special courses, including clinical experience, as an integral part of his preparation for the ministry. Or, he may be an otherwise untrained minister, rabbi, or priest who does the best he can with the tools of compassion, empathy, and patience with which nature and nurture have endowed him.

Clergymen are, of course, consulted about matters of faith and doctrine. Simple and direct answers often suffice. They also deal with religious crises of adolescence and other critical periods, and people are not infrequently helped to replace a childhood set of beliefs with more sophisticated ones. Pastoral counseling can, therefore, revolve about predominantly religious matters.

Some cases are far from simple:

A young woman returned time after time to see a priest about increasingly abstract theological questions. He had to tell her finally that these should not concern her. He recognized "excessive scrupulosity" and advised psychiatric help. He was correct. The persistent doubts and questions turned out to be the beginning symptoms of a schizophrenic illness.

A high school senior, daughter of conventional, middle-class, Methodist parents, was suddenly converted to a highly evangelical religious sect. She believed that the Lord's will directed her every decision so long as she obeyed the leader of the sect. Her parents were distraught but helpless. It was clear that this girl was fearful of graduation and of increasing independence, but at the same time ambivalently rebellious against the authority of her parents. Her "conversion" proclaimed emancipation from the parents but also perpetuated her dependence, only now upon God's will as translated by a self-designated evangelist.

Pastoral counselors may be confronted with situations involving the expression of emotional conflict or psychiatric illness in religious terms or a religious context. When this happens, a pastoral counselor becomes a counselor in the widest sense—a psychotherapist—or else seeks other help. It is the same, of course, in the case of more familiar situations: marital conflicts, problems of personal adjustment, and problems with children.

Some pastoral counselors are becoming a distinct professional group. The American Association of Pastoral Counselors is defining requirements for training and setting standards of competence. It is expected, for example, that a pastoral counseling service will have psychologists and psychiatrists as consultants and supervisors. One such service reports that 60 per cent of its clients come with marital problems, and another 15 to 20 per cent with problems about adolescent children. These family problems, interestingly enough, frequently follow reception of the first high school report card, reflecting a widespread and intense concern about the importance of higher education in the face of automation and a corresponding fear of "dropouts." Strictly religious problems (or religious problems *narrowly* defined) are few in such a counseling service. The ministry assumes new scope and new dimensions, however, and problems of interpersonal and other maladjustments are now sometimes considered religious problems.

Clergymen counselors can sometimes offer immediate service, thereby becoming "crisis clinics." They work with the poor and therefore may regard themselves as the "poor man's psychiatrist." They see those who fear psychiatry lest they be considered "insane" or who avoid a social agency because it may be too remote and out of the regular pattern of their lives. At the same time, however, ministers see clients who are on a waiting list for some agency, clinic, or private resource; or, again, those who have been discharged from hospitals or other treatment, but still feel a need for supportive counseling.

Pastoral counselors also work with other clergymen, individually or in seminars, who are concerned with their own inner tensions, with transference and countertransference aspects of working with parishioners, with how to handle hostility, with how to recognize mental illness, and with a host of other problems that arise whenever people minister to and work with others. Clergymen have always been counselors, of course, but now they are adding professional training to compassion and benevolence.

F. *Counseling and Psychiatric Practice*

The first fact about psychiatric practice is that very much the same kinds of people with the same kinds of problems come to a psychiatrist nowadays as come to clergymen, social workers, clinical psychologists, family doctors, or others in the helping professions. There are differences, however, that arise from the fact that a psychiatrist is not only a physician, but also has had additional intensive training in the field of emotional and mental illnesses, including the most severe. The modern psychiatrist, therefore, is equipped not only to do what we call counseling (from giving advice to intensive psychotherapy), but also to prescribe drugs and to hospitalize patients for whatever therapies are best suited to a given illness.

The psychiatrist, accordingly, is sometimes viewed as the therapist of last resort. He gets patients that other doctors find too difficult or do not have the time to treat. Others are referred to him when counseling (in a limited sense) has failed. Symptoms of marked personality disintegration, such as delusions, hallucinations, severe asocial or antisocial behavior, and depressive reactions with suicidal threats, are likely to evoke a call for psychiatric help. A psychiatrist, then, may have patients who might otherwise have gone to a counselor in another field and he may have patients whom only a physician is equipped to treat, utilizing therapies that only a doctor is legally empowered to administer.

Another fact about psychiatrists is that they themselves specialize. Some limit themselves to hospital practice, others to office practice. Some are predominantly psychotherapists, others favor drug and other organic therapies. The psychotherapy of some, like counseling, is limited to advice, suggestion, and reassurance; that of others is "deeper" and more "intensive," involving concepts and techniques derived from psychoanalysis. About one-tenth of all psychiatrists *are* psychoanalysts, and this creates a situation—as we shall see from the following—that is not without its difficulties.

Therefore, many psychiatrists are skilled in counseling, however this may be defined. They themselves prefer to call it psychotherapy. They have one advantage in diagnosis in that they are better prepared to evaluate other medical conditions that may cause or complicate the patient's problems. They may, however, be overly preoccupied with pathology. Unless they have been well supervised as students, they may be less likely than social workers, for example, to be aware of patients' strengths. Psychiatrists are also in a position to combine psychotherapy with the prescription of, say, tranquilizers. This may be very helpful with some patients, although with others the roles of "medical doctor" and psychotherapist cannot be combined fruitfully.

G. *Counseling and Psychoanalysis*

Psychoanalysis is at least *three* things. It is best known in the popular mind as a *method of therapy*. It is a form of psychotherapy having relatively limited application considering the wide range of human problems and human capabilities. It is, in addition, a *research tool*, an extremely useful device for the intensive study of otherwise unconscious psychological processes. Finally, and by far the most important, it is a *general psychology;* i.e., a set of observations, theories, and laws of human behavior, especially the kinds of human behavior that we call mental functioning. It is particularly important to distinguish psychoanalysis as a body of knowledge (as a psychology, that is) from psychoanalysis as a form of treatment for certain emotional or other psychiatric illnesses.

Psychoanalysis has had such a tremendous impact upon the intellectual life of our time that it is extremely difficult to be objective about it. Despite the cartoons, jokes, and invectives, it has revolutionized our understanding of human personality. All of the psychological and social sciences have had to come to terms with psychoanalytic data and hypotheses. All of the helping professions have adopted such working concepts as unconscious motivation, repression, regression, transference, countertransference, and numerous others. Psychic phenomena, from slips of the tongue to the severest schizophrenia, have been illuminated by psychoanalysis. For all of its theoretical incompleteness, psychoanalysis is probably the most workable and best-integrated account of human behavior currently available to us.

The very force of psychoanalytic psychology has made it difficult to separate it from psychoanalytic treatment. Confusion of the two has led to "status problems" to such a degree that some psychiatrists, for example, have felt it necessary to appear to be psychoanalysts; and social workers, psychologists, and other counselors to ape the formal behavior of psychoanalysts. This kind of identification is often wish-fulfilling, as if one could hope to speak Italian simply by sitting down to an Italian dinner.

There has been a salutary change in recent years. Psychiatrists, social workers, and others who deal with people's problems have learned that they can draw from psychoanalysis in order to enrich their understanding of human personality, but, at the same time, preserve their professional identities and appropriate techniques in their own work with clients or patients. The appropriate application of all that one knows frequently means doing much less than one might like to do, whether because of one's own limitations or those of the client or of his external reality situation. A counselor may say, "I know from experience that I cannot work comfortably with delinquent girls," and this can be no less realistic than for an analyst to say, "Obviously I cannot analyze someone who is dying of cancer." In one instance, *help* means referral to someone else; in the other, it is sharing and support rather than analytic work. In short, psychoanalytic *understanding* should enable us to know when psychoanalytic *techniques* are indicated and when they are not; and this has relevance for our selection of clients or the choice of methods of working with them.

Psychoanalytic treatment, traditionally, is for persons whose neurotic symptoms or restricted lives are primarily the result of intrapsychic conflict. These conflicts are accompanied by overt or potential anxiety that, through defensive efforts, results in disabling symptoms or crippling inhibitions. The analyst endeavors to create a therapeutic situation in which the patient revives and relives the strivings, fantasies, and feelings of earlier years—the transference neurosis—and then, by interpretation and working through, experiences diminution or eradication of neurotic conflicts. This, in brief, is the reason for the analytic setting and the formal behavior of the analyst.

Modifications of the classical view of psychoanalysis put greater emphasis upon the patient's early relationships with parents and others important to him and, therefore, upon an analytic relationship designed to neutralize and counteract the damaging effects of crucial childhood experiences. The greater the shift from considerations of psychic reality and intrapsychic conflict to interpersonal relationships and conflicts, for example, between parents and children, the greater the shift from classical psychoanalysis to other forms of psychotherapy, including what may occur in counseling. Related considerations include how thoroughly the therapist works with childhood determinants of present problems and whether (or how much) he works with transference.

The psychoanalyst, then, does very little counseling *per se*. In classical analysis, the only counseling the patient gets —except at times of crisis—is the initial recommendation to undergo analysis. The psychoanalyst, in other words, seldom makes suggestions or gives advice. Ideally he limits himself, once treatment has begun, to listening, calling the patient's attention to the implications of what he has said (confrontation), asking an occasional question, and making interpretations. The patient's ego, if the preliminary diagnosis has been correct, is strong enough to use constructively the insights of the analytic work and to deal independently with its own life situation apart from the analysis.

H. *Counseling in Other Settings*

Obviously, counseling occurs in many other settings. Management consultants, trust officers, personnel workers,

visiting nurses, and a legion of others encounter daily opportunities for counseling and are often compelled to undertake it. A highly specialized Chicago surgeon once estimated
that 75 per cent of his patients had psychiatric—i.e., emotional—problems. He saw the need but had neither the time
nor the training to do much more than deplore the fact.

This, of course, points to still another problem, for the
need is everywhere but relatively little can be done to meet
it. Facilities are very limited even for those who ask for help
and relatively few who could use help ask for it. Every
neighborhood includes individuals and families who might
benefit from counseling or other treatment, but only a frac-
tion of these are aware of the need; and only a small percentage will take steps to do something about it.

One aspect of the fact that counseling is available in different places by individuals of different professional training
needs further study. This is the matter of the client's choice
of person and of place. And what does the client openly or
tacitly expect of the "brand" of counselor that he has
chosen?

In many instances such questions have little relevance.
The choice of counselor may be determined by convenience, propinquity, rumor, recommendation of a friend, or
previously established relationship as with a doctor, clergyman, attorney, or employer. There are, so to speak, certain
"natural choices" that need little further explanation.

Nevertheless, a client's expectations are likely to be determined to some extent by the person and the profession of
the counselor of his choice. There will always be some measure of anticipatory "set" or transference. The person who
selects his family doctor, for example, will expect not only
a "medical approach" to his problems but also a measure of
parental solicitude, understanding, and omnipotence. More
than this, he may unconsciously hope to find a "physical

reason" for his troubles rather than some other explanation. There are reasons for asking, in any event, to what extent the course of counseling or other therapy is determined by the manner in which clients relate themselves to different individuals in different professions, as well as to what extent the outcome is affected by how the latter, with differences in training and experience, work with clients.

Unrealistic or other special expectations are generally handled by interpretation. This is not always possible or even desirable, however, as the following vignette suggests:

> A young woman with many serious problems and crumbling defenses was referred by a Catholic priest to a non-Catholic counseling agency. She was involved in crisis after crisis and had little tolerance of self-inspection. The need for counseling was clear enough, but it was the consultant's opinion that this must include considerable "environmental manipulation." Specifically, he wondered if the priest who had, if anything, been too permissive, might not deal with his charge in a somewhat firmer way, thus taking the place of an authoritarian father (whom the girl was missing badly) and hopefully thus alleviate the emotional depression that was a source of critical concern.

It is reasonable to ask: Did this client turn to the priest in the first place partly because of her need for parental firmness?

Lewis Hill once wrote an article setting forth the unconscious reasons why his patients selected him to be their analyst. It is seldom possible to know such answers in detail. Clients will sometimes choose a Jewish agency, for example, because they expect to be better understood there, but others will avoid the sectarian resource because they are ashamed of their difficulties or because they do not wish to be identified with its clientele. To be known as a "Christian psychiatrist," to cite another example, is regarded as a boon by some, but by others as a cross to be borne. Clients may select on such a basis hoping for greater sympathy, wanting double benefits of religion and therapy, assuming that they can avoid "dirty" subjects or wishing to avoid having, as they fear, their religious beliefs tampered with. Frequently enough, it is just the "dirty" subjects that should be dealt with, or it is the client's religious doubts that plague him, so that this kind of reaching out for help carries with it built-in defenses against consideration of tender subjects that are most germane.

This is a time of much concern about the "public image" of the several helping professions. Perhaps this is important. Whatever the successes of public relations experts, however, there are bound to be many images in the eyes and minds of clients. Unconscious as well as conscious needs and strivings will dictate how they view the counselors to whom they turn for help. The moral, in brief, is this: The fact that a client turns to one individual or to one profession can rarely be an occasion for self-congratulation on the part of the counselor.

I. *Counseling Techniques*

No matter who a counselor is, what his training, or where he works, four principal tools are available to him for helping clients. They will be listed here, and briefly discussed, because they are generic in counseling. Used intuitively by some, they are consciously employed by others more highly trained. To be effective they must be used appropriately, and this is where native skill and tact, as well as training and experience, count heavily.

Relationship is the basic tool of counseling. Because of its powerful, pervasive strengthening effect, when wisely used, it is also called *supportive relationship*. The force of relationship is based upon the counselor's closeness, sharing, acceptance, understanding, and strength. What the counselor supplies, in other vocabularies, is *caritas* or love. Its prototype is parental love. It says, in effect, "I will listen; I will try to understand; I will accept you as you are; I will share with you your anxiety, guilt, shame, and other concerns; I will sit with you as you reveal your anguish; I will draw you out; I will suggest possibilities for you without dictating or taking over what can only be *your* life and *your* decisions; I will, in short, offer you a controlled friendship that demands nothing of you for myself but that, hopefully, will sustain and strengthen you until you can sustain yourself."

There is the possibility of such emotional support in all human relationships. We all know what builds us up or tears us down. The boss compliments a secretary and she exclaims: "He made my day!" It is much the same wherever there is admiration, respect, friendship, or love. It differs in counseling in that it must be limited and appropriate; that it is dedicated to therapeutic goals; and that its use is directed to the ultimate separation of the client from the counselor. In some respects it is more deeply satisfying for the client than a good marriage and more bitterly frustrating than a bad one, and by definition it is pledged to culminate in "divorce."

Another vignette:

A relief client stopped to cash a small check and was handed the money in a perfunctory manner. Leaving the bank, he said to himself, "If that's the way they feel about me they can have their lousy dough." Acting upon this feeling, he returned to confront the cashier only to find her smiling warmly at him. She acknowledged that she had been hurried and stated that the bank appreciated his patronage. This made *his* day, as he told his caseworker, and it dissolved for the moment the extremely sensitive and paranoid feelings connected with his being on relief.

These examples of support in everyday life can only indicate what a counselor does deliberately. It is not false because it springs from a fundamental liking and respect for people. It is used or made manifest, however, in accordance with its appropriateness. It comprises attitudes and actions as well as spoken words that convey a sense of warmth, build up self-esteem, indicate acceptance, and generally create an emotional climate in counseling that fosters self-respect, self-reliance, and other ego strengths. Elements of a supporting relationship—encouragement, sympathy, reassurance, praise, and so on—are detrimental only when they are false or offered when unneeded and unwanted. Unless the counselor is quite sure of the client's emotional situation, he had better sit quietly by while the client struggles with his problem. This, indeed, may be all the support that is really indicated.

The counseling relationship supplies strengths to the client because of his inevitable transferences to the counselor. The doctor, the clergyman, and other helping persons are from the outset somewhat Olympian figures in the eyes of a worried and anxious client. One young, inexperienced, and inwardly tremulous physician was astounded to discover that an older patient's very respectful behavior arose from the fact that he reminded her of an always impressive grandfather with whose qualities she had unconsciously endowed him. These magical attributes of omniscience and omnipotence are usually enhanced, as the experience of the counselor's acceptance and understanding evokes the client's deeper trust and feeling of security. The prototype, again, is that of the insecure and helpless child drawing support and strength from its wise and powerful parents.

Manipulation of the environment is another important therapeutic tool of counselors. This comprises whatever environmental changes can be effected to remove or alleviate what, for the client, are sources of stress. Such maneuvers range from recommending a visiting nurse for a young and inexperienced mother to placing a badly rejected child in a sympathetic foster home.

The dangers of unnecessary and excessive manipulation are obvious. They subvert a client's strengths. Infantilizing interferences of any sort must always be avoided. Counseling implies exploration of the client's fundamental preferences and potentialities to the end that these, rather than the tastes or predilections of the counselor, determine what, if any, environmental changes should be made.

It was once argued that British working-class families should not be provided with new housing because they would only store their coal in the bathtubs. This is a highly dubious argument against environmental change. By the same token, however, poor housing might be the best solution for an elderly couple who would fall apart if forced to change. We are likely to have very strong feelings, pro or con, about taking young children away from, say, delinquent mothers. It can be hard to remember that it is not the character of the mother but the quality of the mothering that counts so far as children are concerned. In any case, counselors should not rush into such situations, and suggested changes must ordinarily be thoroughly discussed with the client before definitive steps are taken.

Clarification is another technical device of counseling relationships. One aspect of <u>clarification is that of defining a problem.</u> This is an important theme in initial interviews. Closely related to this is putting the problem into perspective by exploring with the client whether it is less serious or more serious than it first appears. Another type of clarification continues throughout the counseling relationship. This includes seeing various ramifications and implications of a problem and, particularly, assisting the client to separate out its objective and external elements from the internal, subjective factors that distort his judgment and militate against constructive solutions. An amputee, for example, must often be helped to distinguish his realistic limitations from those imposed by his inner feeling that he is worthless or by the (unconscious) conviction that he is being punished for his sins.

A brief example of clarification follows:

A young married man sought counseling because of excessive drinking and threatened disruption of his marriage. He soon revealed (1) an endocrine problem requiring new evaluation; (2) insecurity about his masculinity and sexual adequacy; (3) a pattern of unnecessary overwork such that he seldom saw his wife; (4) evidence that the wife's hours of work were likewise unnecessarily long; and (5) indications of stress reactions to the limited and narrow environment of the far northern outpost where they lived.

The counselor did little more than indicate the importance of follow-up for these problems. He asked, "Can you get a comparable job within striking distance of the facilities you need?" This by itself served as clarification and, perhaps, permission. The client revealed that, in fact, he had been offered an excellent job in a place where he would enjoy living, where his wife could pursue more of her interests, and where medical and counseling facilities would be close by. He had been so weighted down with anxiety, shame, and guilt about his symptoms that he failed to see solutions that he had almost worked out by himself.

Finally, there is *interpretation*. This involves comments on the client's feelings, actions, or ways of thinking. It makes him aware of something previously unknown to him or successfully ignored. It also supplies a reason.

Interpretation therefore goes beyond clarification or confrontation. The latter might take the form of pointing out to a client that he habitually escapes from difficult situations by fantasy or wishful thinking. "You are always doing thus and so" is confrontation or clarification. Interpretation takes the further step of adding: "Because . . ." and the "because" is a reason or a motive of which the client is unconscious. Effective interpretation is geared to the material of the interviews and carries emotional as well as intellectual conviction. If the conditions for such acceptance do not exist, the client will brush off the interpretation as perhaps an interesting observation, if true.

Interpretation is the major tool of psychoanalysis. Its use in counseling is much debated. It is certainly possible in counseling to help the client become aware of things he has forgotten or conveniently chosen to ignore, but this is not likely to occur with things that have been deeply repressed. There are many semantic difficulties here and they must be left to other writers. For present purposes it is enough to state that the counselor can successfully interpret and make conscious what has been *preconscious* (a degree of unawareness), but can seldom recover what is *unconscious* in the sense of repressed and stoutly defended against. Much depends, however, upon what it is that has been repressed and how long and strong the defenses are against its becoming conscious.

Reasons for avoiding an arbitrary position about these matters are indicated by the following experiences:

(*a*) A girl, home from a date, said, "Good night, John." The boy replied, "My name's Bill, remember?" The embarrassed girl knew well enough the preconscious wish behind her slip. She had wanted John to call and had reluctantly accepted the date with Bill. The slip, so quickly called to her attention, brought back feelings she had put aside. Still unconscious, because deeply buried were feelings from early childhood that influenced her preference for John.

An intermediate situation might arise in counseling, if the counselor's name is John. Such a slip betrays a wish to have a date with him or to have Bill be like her image of her counselor. Coming out in an interview, such material invites a transference interpretation.

(*b*) A young man in therapy was jilted some months earlier. Currently he reports going to the airport with another girl. Leaving the airport, she said teasingly, "You certainly snubbed your old friend, Mary." The client, startled, realized that he had indeed seen Mary, but without conscious recognition. His tense and perplexed recounting of the episode made interpretation easy: He had unconsciously suppressed a full awareness of Mary's presence both as a defense against the recent hurt and as an indirect expression of an unconscious vindictive wish to obliterate her altogether.

(*c*) A very shy young Navy enlisted man finally "popped the question" and set a date to be married while on leave. Suddenly all leaves were canceled and he was back on sea duty filled with anger, frustration, and longing for his fiancée. He expressed these feelings in violent masturbation, only to be plagued with nightmares of bloody personal injury and intense masturbation guilt. When this became intolerable, he ran amok and slashed lines and hoses about the ship. Then, as he was apprehended, he cut his wrist.

He appeared schizophrenic when seen by a medical officer. He nevertheless poured out the story of his frustrated plans and his bitter resentment of the Navy. The officer absorbed the angry outburst and pointed out how these feelings went into the masturbation which the young man then felt had to be severely punished. As the officer alluded to the symbolic nature of the ropes and hoses, the man unconsciously covered his wounded wrist with the other hand. When both noted this gesture, the officer said quietly, "See what I mean?" He did not say, " 'If thy right hand offend thee . . .' " but the patient got the point, and he was apparently well from that point on. Most cases, of course, are less dramatic, but the *principles* of interpretation are the same.

(*d*) A twenty-one-year-old college girl came for counseling because all of her friends were getting engaged while she herself had never had a date. Interviews revealed that her ways of relating to others were bizarre and paradoxical. She spoke almost in whispers, gave unexpected responses to ordinary greetings, and was generally stilted and overintellectual. Later, she expressed fears of being trapped or engulfed in relationships.

What could be interpreted eventually was that these

odd ways of responding to others were defensive maneuvers and self-defeating. Behind the fears that she was aware of were other fears of sexuality and of successful competition with a less attractive sister and unhappy mother. Fantasies of violent angry outbursts could be interpreted as a reason for whispered conversations. Such interpretations did not delve deeply into childhood determinants or involve anything not easily available to consciousness in the security of a counseling relationship.

Effective interpretation, appropriately timed, informs the client of his defenses and of the reasons for them. What has been demonstrated, however, is that previously unconscious feelings, thoughts, and other behaviors can become conscious spontaneously, or in the course of normal conversation or, in counseling, by interpretation. Such interpretation usually releases what has been preconscious as contrasted to what has been long repressed and, in this sense, deeply unconscious. Interpretation is effective, finally, when the client can almost make it by himself on the basis of thoughts and feelings emerging in the counseling relationship and providing insights previously warded off by patterns of social functioning or by other effective but not too rigid defenses.

J. Summary and Rules of Thumb

We have boldly asserted that many of the principles, techniques, and goals of physicians, clergymen, social workers, clinical psychologists, and others helping clients with personal problems are those of counseling. Distinctions from casework, psychotherapy, or other treatment programs based principally upon relationship and psychological communication are distinctions without much difference. Indeed, these terms are largely interchangeable.

The term *counseling* is employed here chiefly because it is most widely used among the numerous professional groups that provide such services. These services are expanding and multiplying, and greater numbers of professional persons in various disciplines are being trained as counselors. Their basic training *as counselors*, apart from other professional education, is becoming increasingly uniform as to fundamental understanding of human personality and carefully supervised clinical experience prior to independent practice.

Here are some rules of thumb that apply to most counseling situations:

1. Counseling takes time. The client cannot be hurried into feelings of trust and freedom to reveal what to him are painful topics. The "fifty-minute hour" is not simply a convenience. It suits the needs and natural rhythm of many counselors and clients.

2. Counseling requires privacy and relative freedom from distractions. Avoid telephone calls and other interruptions. Both client and counselor need relative continuity for the most effective interaction.

3. Taking notes is inimical to listening. Unless facts are of the highest value—legal data, for example—empathic impressions are better. A counselor will more surely notice important connections and themes in a client's material if not preoccupied with taking notes.

4. A counselor listens and avoids unnecessary talk. He makes it easy for the client to talk, and keep on talking. He is cheerful, affable and encouraging in

manner, but with economy of words. There is no need for stony, staring silence.

5. It is unnecessary to organize everything or find out the meaning of every small detail. Note first of all the broad canvass of the client's personality and story and then predominant themes in what he has to say. The counselor's own reflections, as the client talks, are frequently of the highest relevance as clues to what is most important.

6. Be sure about the meanings of important words and phrases. "A few drinks" can mean two drinks or a pint. "Moderate exercise" varies from once around the block to three sets of tennis. "My husband is an alcoholic" sometimes means that he goes to the tavern on Saturday night.

7. A physician has an especially vital counseling role in discussing the results of examinations or advising medical or surgical procedures. These can be highly mysterious even to intelligent and educated laymen. A federal judge is capable of asking if the uterus lies underneath the liver! A patient needs careful explanations and frequently repeated explanations. Intense anxiety prevents "seeing" and "hearing." He needs time, also, to work through and set straight whatever is stirred up by a diagnosis or treatment procedure.

8. A counselor's questions should be clearly and carefully worded. Frequently they should be openended in order to invite discussion and to avoid monosyllabic and final "yes" or "no" responses. "How did you feel when you left your family?" is generally better, for example, than "Did you feel

guilty when you left your family?" The latter is a leading question that sounds like an accusation. Later on, however, if the client struggles for a word, one might say, "Did it feel like sorrow or shame or guilt?" At other times one must have exact data, and the questions must be correspondingly precise. It is frequently useful to let the client tell his story in his own way for one or several interviews and then, by necessary questions, fill in missing details of his developmental history or the onset and development of the problems he has been referring to.

9. If humanly possible, see clients by appointment and be on time. Structuring of formal arrangements for interviews as to time, place, duration, fees, and related matters provides an important base line. Provided the counselor is faithful to what has been agreed upon, deviations by the client are important indexes as to what is otherwise unexpressed by him. Beyond this, people who are kept waiting, or who in other ways are confronted with the unexpected, become more anxious and angry with each passing minute. An entire clinical picture can be changed by feelings that build up in a "waiting room."

CHAPTER TWO

The Initial Interview

The initial interview is the first coming together of a professional helping person and another person wanting some kind of service. This may be their only meeting or the first of several. Possibly it is the first of hundreds. The initial interview differs from all others, however, in that these two strangers have to get acquainted and, most of all, they must find out if they can talk to one another.

The client may be an old hand at asking for help and outlining his problems. He may be inexperienced and very anxious. The counselor, on his part, has to form his impressions of this new client. The situation therefore comprises the usual elements of forming a new acquaintance, plus those of mutual evaluation, as the client asks himself, "Will this person be able to understand and help me?" while the counselor silently considers, "Will I be able to understand and work with this individual?"

Almost any initial interview will contain some or many of the following elements:

The client comes because of a marital problem. He has experienced or had fantasies about infidelity, sepa-

33

ration, or divorce. He feels *guilty* about some of his behavior, *ashamed* about his failure, *defensive* about real or expected social disapproval, *angry* at the actual or anticipated vindictiveness of his spouse, *worried* over the effects upon the children, and *depressed* about the whole situation and his prospects for the future.

On top of this, he is *ashamed* at having to confess all of this to a stranger, *doubtful* as to what will come of it, *suspicious* about the confidentiality of the relationship, *hostile* in the face of expected judgmental attitudes, and generally *guarded* about the whole procedure. He would not be there, however, if he were not *desperate* about the situation, *hopeless* about solving it himself, *hopeful* that the counselor can come up with something useful and that he can get some *relief* by unburdening his feelings.

All of this—and more!—will determine the content and emotional climate of the initial interview.

A. *Getting Started*

The counselor encounters first the client's social personality, his healthy ego. This begins with some kind of formal introduction. It is frequently enough to greet the client in the reception room or other meeting place, and then add, "I am Mr. Smith. My office is this way." Or, "We can talk in here." Once settled, the following is usually quite enough: "Well, will you tell me what brings you here?" Obviously this would not be tactful if the answer would have to be, "My mother!"

The point is, however, that most clients have anxiously built themselves up for this moment and want only a friendly and dignified invitation to start talking. There is quite likely to be defensive blocking, joking, testing, or other delaying tactics. This is apt to be short-lived if the counselor refrains from becoming overly involved. If the client is largely passive or uncooperative, it may be necessary for the counselor to take much of the initiative. He may discover, for example, that the client is there under protest, that it really wasn't *his* idea, or that he is overly awed by class, status, or educational differences—actual or imagined.

The following example will indicate the need for flexibility:

A seven-year-old boy is taken to a counselor because of reading difficulties at school. He rushes into the office carrying a sheaf of his drawings and paintings, and immediately starts displaying these. This is the child's way of putting his best foot forward. His behavior says: "I may not be so good at reading, but I can draw and paint."

Adults have their ways of accomplishing the same purpose. The wise counselor will accept this defense by expressing interest in the client's abilities and strengths, but will tactfully bring the discussion around to the more pertinent reasons for the interview. This may be done in five minutes or forty-five. It may even be postponed to a subsequent appointment, but sooner or later, when the client feels accepted for himself, the focus must be where it belongs.

The question of timing is not easy. If the counselor postpones the inevitable confrontation too long, the client's anxiety will increase. After all, *he* knows why he is there and it cannot help if he feels that the counselor is afraid of coming to grips with the problem. One must therefore respect a client's defenses, but for no longer than is absolutely necessary.

Here is another first encounter:

> A young woman client came late to her first appointment. Given free rein to talk, she was soon looking out the window and speaking of her wish to travel in foreign countries. Her manner was diffident and it was clearly difficult for her to talk. Evidently she was saying, although indirectly, "I wish I were almost anywhere but here."

This kind of defense can be picked up immediately. The counselor must be kind about it, but quite direct. He should agree that it is difficult to be here and add that the client naturally prefers thinking about the pleasures of foreign travel rather than dealing with unpleasant realities closer to home. Such an interpretation in an initial interview may lose an occasional client, but it will save many more for continued counseling.

The "initial interview" sometimes takes a number of appointments, as the following indicates:

> The young mother of three infants, each about a year apart, came for financial aid because of the apparent desertion of her husband. A short time later, however, the husband returned. When he was seen by the counselor, he complained of the noise and confusion at his place of work. It "gets me down," he said. "I just had to take off for a few days." The counselor established the fact that he was "nervous and high-strung." The treatment plan was to move toward referral to a psychiatrist.

This plan was premature. The counselor should have heard the client out. He "took off" from home as well as from work, and it seems obvious where the noise and confusion were most trying. His feelings about three infant children and a chronically tired wife should have been explored. Neither he nor the counselor had anything to lose from a discussion of the population explosion at home and what, if anything, might be done to make conditions more tolerable. Psychiatric referral, if indicated, can be deferred where situational factors are so obvious, assuming that there are no other signs of psychiatric illness than the ones described.

A client may defend against anxiety by being disruptive or attacking. Such defenses are hard to take, but less so if one anticipates them. It is remarkable what major changes can occur between a first and second interview. A client who first appears on the verge of tantrum or collapse may come a second time collected and ready to go to work.

In the following instance there was no second interview:

A young couple came to the office with their infant. When asked to come into the interviewing room, the husband picked up the crying baby and brought her along. He then addressed the counselor, who was twice his age, in most familiar terms. The counselor, reacting to the disruption of the interview and the uncalled for intimacy as an attack, was furious. He could not be objective and there was no basis for further work.

This was a complicated situation and the client was undoubtedly provocative. The counselor, however, should have understood the client's familiarity as a "testing" and his bringing in the baby as a symptomatic act. The young man may have wished to call attention to the infant in himself or, by being so parental, to deny such strivings or to reveal the maternal side of his personality, or simply to distract attention from his problems. Whatever it was, the counselor should have tried to understand, instead of reacting as disruptively himself.

The picture of a strong and reassuring counselor greeting a quaking and needy client suggests gross inequalities in the relationship. It is true that the client comes with a problem and is expected to reveal much about himself, while the counselor has certain skills to offer and will remain relatively anonymous. The inequalities are, however, frequently quite circumscribed. The client may, for example, be a prostitute or a United States Senator and may therefore know considerably more about sex or politics than the counselor; may, indeed, know more about "life" and human nature than the counselor. It is well to be modest about such matters, remembering at the same time that the client has his specific needs in *this* situation and the counselor his specific skills. What counts are not the inequalities, such as they are, but rather whether—in *this* professional relationship—there can be a useful accommodation of needs and services.

B. *What to Look For*

The most important consideration of the first interview is this: Is the client in the right place? A preliminary diagnostic formulation is therefore in order. Diagnostic problems will be the subject of a later chapter but it is important to state at once that diagnostic activity begins with the first meeting with the client and can result in the initial interview being the only one.

The client has troubles and what he wants initially are some answers. What do his troubles amount to and what can be done about them? He is not versed in the ways of counseling. If he knew the proper terminology he would request a consultation. Counseling, if indicated, will have to be explained to him. It usually takes time to shift an urgent appeal for help, clouded as it is with intense, conflicting emotions, to a problem-solving context. From the client's point of view, the first order of business is something like this: What is wrong? Do I have cancer? Am I going crazy? Will my husband leave me? Is it my fault? Next in order is: Can something be done? Can you help me? And finally: Well, then, how do we go about it?

The counselor and the client must examine together what it is that brings the client to the counselor. This entails a detailed consideration of the client's difficulties as *he* views them, together with some exploration of whether his expectations are realistic or unrealistic. This, in turn, must take into account the hopes and expectations that may be unrealistic for *this* particular counselor or agency or may be unrealistic for *any* available resource. For example, it is unrealistic for a client to demand that a social worker tell him if certain symptoms are psychosomatic, just as it is unrealistic for him to insist that *any* counselor make crucial life decisions for him. The latter part of an initial interview is likely to be occupied with clarification of just such matters and it is up to the counselor to be quite clear and firm about them. Untold time and effort are not uncommonly wasted when a counselor becomes preoccupied with "building a relationship" before establishing in his own mind whether the relationship is indicated, or before deciding with the client what it can hope to accomplish and what its formal arrangements are to be.

Another question for the counselor is: Who *is* the client? This is a diagnostic problem that cannot be long deferred. Women come in frequently complaining about their alcoholic husbands and the chaos in the home. They hope somehow to involve the husband in getting treatment. This is certainly a disturbing situation, but it is occasionally complicated by the fact that the unhappy woman unconsciously encourages and facilitates the very problem that she is consciously so upset about. It will be difficult to involve the husband before the woman can understand her contribution to his problem.

The mother who brings a pregnant teen-age daughter for help is not uncommonly in a comparable predicament. The parental relationship and its repercussions for the daughter can be a major factor in the daughter's problems. Often as not, the parents must look at themselves if the daughter is to be helped.

Considerations such as these set limits to the diagnostic thinking of the first interview. They give us pause because they open up the possibility that there may be several clients, not just the designated or self-appointed one. If this is likely to be so, it should be indicated to the client who makes the original contact. If this is not feasible, it should be pointed out, tactfully to be sure, that only limited goals are realistic. The balance of emotional forces within a family is frequently a neurotic one, and change for the better on the part of one individual can mean change for the worse on the part of the others. The issue is sometimes as stark as this: Do we treat one member of a family and let the chips fall as they may, or do we bend our efforts to treating the whole family and hopefully arrive at a healthier balance, but at all cost preserving the integrity of the family?

Here we recapitulate to emphasize some other points. It is generally agreed that the client gets the first chance to talk. Upset or not, he comes with a problem and he has somehow brought himself to a readiness to talk about it. He has formulated his difficulties to the best of his ability, and it is at this point that counseling must start. We have made the point, however, that the first phase of counseling is consultation, a preliminary exploratory phase before commitment to definitive treatment.

The counselor must be willing, within reasonable limits, to hear the client out. Granted that the story may be a tissue of rationalizations and unconscious fabrications, it is a beginning. It enables the counselor to begin the diagnostic task. The client gets some relief from telling it. The counselor notes not only the client's statement of the problem but also his feelings, accusations, defensiveness, evasions, and omissions. He gauges the client's intelligence, his ego strengths and weaknesses, and his probable capacity for using counseling or other services. He knows that the client needs his defenses and that this is not the time to challenge them severely, if at all. The counselor follows a basic rule of therapy: *primum non nocere* (first of all do no harm).

What one looks for, accordingly, are the following: What is it that brings the client for help? Does his formulation of the problem correspond to the counselor's preliminary diagnostic impression? Is the client's request for service realistic (granting that there are always some unconscious magical expectations)? Is he in the right place for the help he needs? What seem to be his strengths? His areas of vulnerability? His indications of resistance, his defenses? All of this may appear to be too much for a single interview, and indeed it may be; but not as a *preliminary, tentative* picture of the client and his difficulties.

C. *An Example*

In the example that follows, *you* are a male counselor of about forty, working in a family agency, and *she*, the client, is a young woman of twenty-three. What transpires would vary somewhat, of course, if you were a physician or a minister, if you were twenty-five, if you were female, and so on. The example indicates something of what goes on subjectively, as well as what more obviously occurs.

The face sheet tells you before you even see the client that she is twenty-three, Roman Catholic, born in Chicago, now living in a suburb of your city (not Chicago), and employed in an office at $350 per month. Your conscious or unconscious diagnostic thinking rules out marital conflicts, feeblemindedness, school problems, conditions found only in hospitals, and various others. You may think of pregnancy, premarital panic, social isolation, or other difficulties most commonly encountered in young, unmarried female adults. You may draw other inferences from your knowledge of where the client works, employment standards for the type of work she does, and whether her salary indicates a superior, average, or inferior position considering the employment situation at the time.

At this point you go out to meet your client. You are introduced by the receptionist or introduce yourself. You behave more or less as you would in meeting anyone new, except that you avoid a first-name approach. You note that the girl is quite good-looking and you remind yourself that you are nearly old enough to be her father. She, meanwhile, takes in a few details about you—probably less flattering than you might wish—or, if she is quite anxious, may not really see you at all despite an adequate social facade. In any case, you show her the way to your office, indicate a chair, shut the door, and initiate a conversation.

During these social amenities you have noted a few things beyond the fact that your client is pretty. She is well-groomed, apparently worried, seemingly shy, and yet not conspicuously ill at ease. Her expression and general demeanor suggest intelligence and at least a modicum of *savior faire*. Your diagnostic appraisal continues: She comes in on her own volition and is apparently well-motivated. If there is any kind of mental or emotional illness she can, at least, keep up appearances and necessary controls. Whatever the problems, there are significant strengths. Everything is within normal limits, thus far, for a person coming into a strange situation and about to ask for some kind of help.

By now the client has asked you if it is OK to smoke, and you have said, "Certainly." Or else she has simply looked at you expectantly and you have asked her what brings her to the agency. You are launched upon some kind of conversation and some kind of relationship. She tells you, haltingly, that she does not know just what the matter is. She has not felt right for several months. She had some counseling in Chicago and was advised to have more after she got settled here. You note to yourself that this is not entirely a new situation and that her problem is not urgent because she was able to wait until she got settled here and found a job. You then ask her to tell you about the earlier counseling experience and what led up to it.

About a year ago, she tells you, she suddenly developed headaches and felt depressed. At about the same time she lost confidence in herself. She does not articulate clearly and you have to strain to hear her. This annoys you, but you counteract your feeling by wondering what it means. Prior to this time, she continues, she was busy and happy. True, there were lots of problems at home, but much of her life was away from home. She does not know if there is any connection, but she became engaged a couple of months before her symptoms began. Also, her father committed suicide two years before that, at which time her mother "went to pieces" and had to be committed for a while. During that period the client had much more responsibility at home where there were several younger siblings, but she has had much more freedom during the past year or so. She has had some doubts about getting married. She values her independence and is afraid that she might feel held down. You note at this point that the parents must have been rather fragile reeds, and yet that this girl functioned adequately until after she got engaged.

By now you have these preliminary impressions: The girl needs help, but she is not in panic. She attempted a solution in leaving Chicago, but it has not worked as well as she had hoped. She may need some support from you but she needs more, in all probability, to explore her reactions to becoming engaged. What does she stand to lose if she gets married? What does she feel she will be getting into?

You note in passing that she has said nothing at all about her fiancé. There is no indication of religious differences or of her own relationship to the Church. She must be running from something, but how much of it is within herself?

You can support her in her feeling that her symptoms indicate underlying problems. She should, however, have a thorough physical examination as a check on the headaches. You and she can explore together her feelings about marriage and try to get at the root of her feelings of depression. What both of you need to do now is to talk about the practical arrangements: Can she come in once a week? Can she come at one of the times you have available? Would she prefer to wait for an opening at another time? What fee is reasonable for her, considering her income after routine expenses? When these matters are disposed of, you send her on the way with something like, "Good-bye. I'll see you a week from Monday at four."

D. *Some Debatable Points*

The first interview should be conducted on the assumption that it may be the only interview. Some writings on the initial interview assume a continuing relationship with the person who first sees the client. How often is this the case? Even if it is, there may be a long waiting period before treatment time (as contrasted to a few diagnostic interviews) is available. In a clinic or agency there may be assignment to another counselor after intake. And, of course, it frequently happens that the client must be referred elsewhere. There are many reasons for avoiding "getting in too deep" at the outset, and these reasons must be made clear to the client in order to forestall deep feelings of disappointment and rejection.

Apart from these considerations, however, both the client and the counselor must have the freedom to decide that they cannot or should not work together. The initial interview explores not only the facts of the client's presenting problems, but the additional fact of compatibility—or lack of it —between client and counselor. The initial interview is therefore a consultation, and there may be others. If these establish the appropriateness of the persons, the problems, and the available resources, then the basis for continued counseling exists. There are, of course, exceptional instances in which consultation takes five minutes and counseling another thirty to forty-five.

Because the initial interview is consultation, it is better to be professional than unduly friendly. One may have a relaxed and friendly manner, to be sure, but it is a mistake to set out to build a friendship. The client comes for help, and what he seeks is skill, tact, awareness, and understanding. These are more reassuring to him than friendliness which, in any case, may be synthetic. Besides, friendliness places him under an obligation to reciprocate, and he may be in no mood even to be nice. If the client decides to continue with the counselor, it will be more because he trusts his competence and understanding than because of any well-intentioned friendliness. Finally, as noted previously, the client must feel free not to continue, and the counselor has no business making such a decision difficult.

"Treatment begins in the first interview." If this is so, it is (usually) a mistake. The first interview may very well be therapeutic, but this is quite another matter. Here again the functions of a consultation take first priority. The client must be free to accept a treatment plan or to reject it, to trust the counselor, or to look elsewhere. He may feel much better after one interview and decide that he needs no more. He might even be relieved of a great burden of anxiety or guilt and still decide that he would prefer another therapist. He may, again, feel much worse and thereby decide that another counselor can help him more effectively.

There must be the basis of a *therapeutic alliance* before formal treatment begins. This means that the counselor has the time and that the client wishes to continue with him. It means also a mutual understanding about hours, fees, and related practical details. But none of this negates the fact that the counselor can be very helpful, during this preliminary period, in sharing the client's anxiety, letting him "blow off steam," helping to delineate the problem, discussing resources and techniques for getting help, and thus putting the client on the road that leads to the possibility of solutions.

The amount of the counselor's activity during the initial interview has been the subject of much discussion. Few clients are prepared for the free association interview, richly rewarding as this can be. Many can accept it, however, if its rationale is first briefly explained. At the outset the counselor must engage the client's conscious ego, listening at the same time for anything he may unconsciously reveal. The chief function of this initial consultation is that of provisional evaluation: What are the most pressing problems? Do they involve a serious danger to the client or to others? What further diagnostic work is indicated? Will counseling be the most appropriate treatment? If so, what type? Am I the person to offer it? The counselor gets many answers by careful listening. He can usually afford to wait before filling in the gaps by questioning, but he cannot postpone the diagnostic task indefinitely. Even if the client precipitates the counselor into a succession of crises lasting days or weeks, the latter must somehow find the time to take stock of what is going on, what kind of basic problem he is dealing with, and what is the most valid long-range treatment plan.

The counselor's activity will be determined also by a host of other factors. These include such things as the client's intelligence, social class, ethnic group, referral source, and all of the elements that affect his motivation. A client sent by the police or shamed into coming or there under threat of exposure or divorce is likely to be angry, defensive, and generally uncooperative. If he can be brought around at all, it will take both time and patience. It is not often advisable to persuade a reluctant client, because this involves, in the client's eyes, assumption of full responsibility by the counselor. There are times and circumstances, nevertheless—for example, where "hard core" dependency and isolation breed apathy and despair—when the counselor must be quite active in stimulating a desire for help.

Psychiatric and social work studies show that, as compared with upper-class clients and patients, those from lower-class groups are less well motivated, less likely to follow through, and less likely to have the capacity for insight. There are, moreover, markedly different attitudes about asking for help. Anglo-Saxons, often Calvinistic, feel ashamed about needing help and they tend to be stoical about their difficulties. These of Latin origins, however, are generally much freer both about being dependent and pouring out their troubles without inhibition of their feelings. Jewish clients, due to tradition and social sophistication, often take help as a matter of course, or even demand it as a right.

The counselor is therefore flexibly alert to the client's readiness to ask for help. If the client is voluble, the counselor hears him out; if not, he draws him out. He does what it takes to complete the picture of the difficulties, meanwhile finding a golden mean between shutting the client off or seducing him into visions of solutions and gratifications that the counselor can never promise to fulfill.

Finally, the counselor may have to dispel some of the magical or other impossible expectations the client inevitably brings with him. By means of the transferences of everyday life, the client will unconsciously see the doctor, for example, as a god, or the clergyman as a Divine Healer. Whether physician, clergyman, or other counselor, he has for the client some exceptional powers. The seeds of the earliest relationship with parents are transplanted into this relationship. Deep within himself, the client is a helpless child, and the counselor becomes perforce a potentially loving, accepting, forgiving, wrathful, punishing, rejecting, always judging and always omnipotent parent. One deals with such expectations initially—they are never dispelled entirely!—by realistic discussion of the functions of counseling, its limitations, its procedures, and the fact that it is a "problem-solving process" that cannot promise magical solutions. The counselor does this, knowing at the same time, however, that the client *must* exaggerate the powers of a professional helping person at a time of need, in order to trust him and to sustain hope that cures or other solutions are possible.

There are more superficial images of the counselor that are determined to some extent by his profession. These images influence the client's statement of his problems and the types of solution he expects or fears. A client coming to a clergyman, for example, may see him as a specialist in sin, but also in forgiveness and consolation. He is likely to expect medicine and practical advice from a doctor, permissiveness from a psychiatrist, or formulas for getting better grades from a school guidance counselor. The temptation for the counselor is to rush in with reassuring words as to his benevolence and objectivity. It is better to wait for evidence of the client's unconscious bias and then point it out to him. If this type of clarification is not effective, it may be necessary to state directly: Our approach is problem-solving. The relationship is confidential. We cannot make decisions for you. The whirring noise is not a recording machine. Or, whatever! Such reassurances must, of course, be truthful, and the need for it must become part of the diagnosis.

E. *Not to Take the Client*

The client must feel free not to return. This is a reason, mentioned earlier, for maintaining a professional distance during the initial interview and for really keeping it a consultation. The same considerations are relevant to the fact that the counselor may not wish to continue with the client.

Sometimes the counselor *cannot* do so. This also has been mentioned. The case may be reassigned after intake in an agency. A psychiatric clinic may not accept long-term cases of doubtful prognosis. A guidance clinic may have an arbitrary age limit of sixteen. The client may not meet certain residence or similar requirements. He may be obviously too sick for counseling or other therapy as an outpatient. The counselor may be booked up for weeks ahead and be compelled to serve only as consultant. The problem, once clarified, sometimes requires immediate referral; e.g., a pregnant college girl to a protective service or a confused elderly person to a physician.

There are other reasons not to continue with a client. Some clients really are untreatable. This does not mean that they might not be helped, given all of the right circumstances—unlimited time, easy access to hospital or sanitarium, just the right counselor, and so on—but it does mean untreatable for all practical purposes. A children's worker with the faith of St. Francis and the patience of Job once said that if the twenty-seventh foster home was not just right for a given child, the twenty-eighth or twenty-ninth might be. There are no untreatable clients for such a counselor, but for most of us there are limits of time, energies, and resources, not to mention commitments to others.

Counselors working with outpatients will do well to avoid taking clients who cannot tolerate the normal frustrations of life. Such individuals tend unconsciously to exploit the relationship and to "act out" when denied, and since they are usually unable to tolerate interpretation, there is little therapeutic leverage. Others, such as many schizophrenics and those with certain personality disorders, do badly with insight therapy (interpretations) but benefit considerably from a supportive relationship and discussion of current reality problems. Others, such as clients with perversions, are likely to have little inner urge to change, and come for help only at the behest of friends or the order of a court. Like Juliet, they will speak, yet they will say nothing; and they will seldom change.

Most counselors discover, moreover, that there are certain kinds of people with whom they cannot work, at least not easily. A very benign psychoanalyst of great sensitivity and skill once remarked that he would never attempt to treat an aggressive, acting-out adolescent male. The fact that he was so benign suggests a reason for this decision; the point is, however, that he accepted this limitation. Counselors, like nurses and others in the helping professions, have their unconscious as well as conscious reasons for wanting to help others. Accordingly, they sometimes feel guilty or upset if they cannot work with everyone who comes to them for help. It is better for them and for their clients if they can settle for less perfectionistic goals.

A tendency to overreact to certain problems accounts partly for the following:

A clever and aggressive teen-age boy got a phychiatrist, a probation officer, and a couple of Roman Catholic priests—and nearly a whole community, besides—embroiled in an uproar when he told the probation officer that one of the priests was a homosexual. Meanwhile he told the same story about the probation officer to one of the priests. The probation officer discussed the matter with the chief of police, who was inclined to believe the story, while the priest reported to his superior who was similarly disposed. The psychiatrist who fortunately could be dispassionate about such matters was able, finally, to call a conference of everyone concerned and to demonstrate that the youth was playing one against the other in turn.

The moral is that homosexuality is too hot a subject for some counselors to handle comfortably. That aggressive adolescents are equally so is not news. There is enough work to be done in the world and each of us should feel free to limit himself to what he can do best. Actually, our clients will benefit as much as we ourselves from such a policy.

CHAPTER THREE

Making Diagnoses

A. *General Principles*

Some counselors are taught: First make a diagnosis, then a treatment plan. Others learn: Treatment begins with the initial contact with a client, and diagnosis evolves gradually. If one has to make a choice, the first is preferable. The second often leads to endless frustration and wasted effort on the part of counselor and client alike.

Fortunately one seldom has to make the choice. The diagnostic thinking of the first interview is not definitive, although, as we have seen, there must be some evaluation. Likewise, the first meeting with a counselor may be extremely therapeutic for the client, even though this is not yet part of a treatment plan. It can be helpful to remember that one does not postpone the diagnostic effort but rather that one becomes progressively clearer about it with each succeeding interview. By the same token, one helps the client as much as possible during every interview, remembering at the same time that this includes making an effective early diagnosis before committing oneself or the client to a long-term treatment plan. The *diagnosis* of the first interviews, in substance, is an evaluation sufficiently complete to form the basis for a treatment plan. The *treatment* of these same interviews is largely an incidental therapeutic benefit derived from the relationship and from the fact of going through the preliminaries of working out a treatment plan.

Diagnosis includes getting an increasingly clearer picture of the client as a person, of the client's problems, and of whatever in the client, or in his environment, helps to explain them. A young woman, mentioned earlier, "broke down" soon after she became engaged. She saw no connection between the two events, but the counselor assumed that there might be an important one. This was a tentative, partial diagnosis. If it proved to be true, there remained the further diagnostic problem of explaining such a serious and paradoxical reaction to what one expects to be a joyous event. Such further diagnostic work admittedly takes longer, but another interview or two will surely reveal whether she is in conflict with her Church, feels too immature and unprepared to consider marriage, or has such neurotic anxiety about matters sexual as to be in panic at thoughts of the wedding night. The treatment plan will vary considerably if one of these possibilities proves to be true. The first calls for counseling with clarification, perhaps; the second, for counseling with considerable support; and the third for counseling with interpretation, if not referral for psychoanalysis.

The facts of many initial interviews reveal the impossibility of a rigid separation of diagnostic and therapeutic effects. The normal processes of making a client feel welcome and helping him to define his problems have therapeutic value. If, as in some instances, he is quite anxious, guilty, or suspicious, these symptoms—diagnostic in themselves—have to be treated to some extent before further diagnostic evaluation is possible. Early treatment is not the beginning of a plan to talk regularly or have family counseling or undergo psychoanalysis, but rather to help the client with doubts, confusion, anxieties, and (very often) lack of knowledge about available procedures and resources. It is, in part, the process of supplanting these with some conviction that problems can be defined and clarified and that counselors have specialized ways of offering help with problem-solving.

If one looks at beginning counseling in this way, it is possible to reconcile apparently conflicting points of view. One can helpfully combine diagnostic and therapeutic efforts without binding the client or committing oneself to a continuing relationship. One can "be therapeutic"—within limits—and defer definitive diagnosis. At the same time one must give predominant consideration to diagnostic considerations before embarking upon a comprehensive treatment plan. In many ways, therefore, diagnosis and treatment proceed apace, but in a larger sense a counselor must diagnose before he treats.

B. *What Is a Diagnosis?*

It is already clear that there is a continuous interaction between the counselor's estimate of what is going on with the client and what the counselor thinks should be done about it. The continuing evaluation is diagnosis (although by no means all of it), and the progression of what the counselor does is treatment (although, again, by no means all of *that*). What the client learns about himself and about his situation, how he responds in the relationship with the counselor, and how he reacts to what he learns are equally important aspects of the diagnostic-treatment process.

We mentioned the diagnostic thinking of the initial interview. The counselor notes how the client formulates his problem (the client's diagnosis) and at the same time pays attention to how he functions in this new and somewhat stressful situation, as well as how he adapts himself and relates to the counselor. From the outset, therefore, diagnostic observation includes the person and the problem of the client or, more accurately, the person with his problem. This comprises what the client has to work with as well as what he has to contend with; i.e., his personal strengths and weaknesses, and the environment in which he lives, moves, and has his being. The counselor learns as much as possible about all of these factors, and is not astonished when new facts emerge to change his diagnostic thinking and his treatment efforts.

Suppose, for example, that the young woman whose symptoms apparently began when she became engaged reveals the fact that she is pregnant. The focus of diagnostic thinking shifts immediately. She must be as much upset about the pregnancy as about the implications of engagement, and probably a good deal more. Is one man involved, or two, or more? Whatever the situation, the pregnancy takes precedence, for the moment, over prior personality problems, conflicts about men, or fears of leaving home for marriage. The diagnostic thinking that began with the first glance at the face sheet and the first meeting with the client is therefore subject to continuous revision as new data emerge. These new data, in turn, cause shifts in emphasis and changes in plans as to what to say next, what to explore next, and what to do next in the total diagnostic-treatment configuration.

Having established the principle that we cannot rigidly separate diagnosis from therapeutic activity, and that the helping and problem-solving process begins, just as the relationship between counselor and client begins, with the first interview, let us elaborate in more systematic fashion some of the important elements of diagnostic thinking and exploration that eventually emerge as a definitive diagnosis. These elements, broadly considered, include: (1) the presenting problems; (2) the onset and course of these problems; (3) the significant conflicts; (4) evaluation of the most relevant environmental pressures as well as those attributable chiefly to the personality of the client; and (5) the diagnostic formulation. Inasmuch as some writers do not approve of a diagnostic approach at all, we shall indicate later some of the reasons for this position.

C. *Presenting Problems*

The presenting problems are the client's problems when he first comes for help. They are his reasons for asking someone else to help him. They include also what may be self-evident to the counselor, even though not mentioned by the client. The counselor must reserve judgment about what the client fails to mention, however. It may not be an important problem, it may not be a problem to the client, or it may be something that is so painful to the client that he himself is unaware of it.

Suppose a client complains of marital problems, and it is quite obvious that he has been drinking. The counselor takes note of the client's failure to mention drinking as a problem. It may turn out, however, that the client has just come from an Irish wedding or an office Christmas party, and the alcohol may be the first that he has had in weeks. Again, a client's presenting problem may be that his children are in some sort of trouble at school. After a few minutes, however, he is talking almost exclusively of "in-law troubles." The client has unconsciously shifted the focus of his presenting problem and perhaps pointed to more fundamental sources of the children's difficulties. The counselor may then call the client's attention to the shift and raise a question about including the in-laws with the presenting problem.

A client's and counselor's initial definition of a problem may agree. If the client is, for example, an unmarried, pregnant girl, the pregnancy is the problem. The immediate and pressing concern of both client and counselor is how the girl can get away and have needed care before the pregnancy becomes a matter of common observation. The counselor will provide an emergency service—such as referring the client to a branch of the National Florence Crittenton Homes Association—knowing that further counseling services as well as maternity care will be provided in a group-living situation that is nevertheless strictly confidential so far as the client's usual community is concerned. If the girl does not wish to go away, or if she has some prospects of marrying, counseling naturally takes a different course and, ultimately, counseling about the numerous factors leading to pregnancy out of wedlock may well be indicated. One of the goals of counseling is that of bringing people with problems together with the community resources best suited to help with a particular problem at a given time; and in the case just cited the diagnostic task is the relatively simple one of agreeing upon the most urgent problem and perhaps of making certain that a pregnancy does, in fact, exist. Further diagnostic work belongs to the obstetrician and to those who work with the client in her new milieu.

Other clients present considerably more complicated problems. It frequently happens that a client appears to be completely ignorant as to the reasons for his coming. He presents a picture of vagueness, confusion, and triviality. This may be a product of his anxiety, and the counselor will be wise to use an indirect approach. A question about the client's past life or other more remote matters may get him started. No matter what a client talks about, he is revealing something of himself and his concerns; and recurrent themes and topics in whatever he says will point the way to what is most distressing now. The counselor must remember that the client is not only defending himself from the counselor but also from himself. The problems may be as painful for the client to face within himself as they are to reveal to someone else and, therefore, cannot be brought out clearly in the first interview or, sometimes, for many interviews thereafter. In such a situation the provisional diagnosis is admittedly superficial; something like, "emotional conflicts of some sort; strongly defended; goodness knows what underneath." Inasmuch as the "goodness knows what" can range from marital infidelity to brain tumor, it is highly important to suspend *final* diagnostic judgment.

D. *Onset and Course*

The "onset and course" of whatever brings the client to the counselor is important for the ultimate diagnosis. It is a statement of when and under what circumstances the difficulty began, and everything related to it that has happened since. Again, the focus is upon what the client considers to be his problem, and this can be misleading. To ignore this approach, however, can be equally misleading.

The "onset and course of the present illness" is taken directly from medicine. Any doctor who interned at the Cook County Hospital in Chicago will recall going to the senior surgeon in the middle of the night regarding some patient with acute abdominal pain, and having to answer: When did the patient first feel sick? What did he first complain of? Then, what did he have for breakfast the day before? For lunch? For dinner? Did the pain move? Did it change in character? It boiled down to a minute-by-minute, blow-by-blow account of the patient's life from a time well before the symptoms began to the time of bringing the case to the surgeon's attention. In other than surgical conditions, such a history can be equally revealing of important correlations and connections. It must not, of course, distract the counselor from the total personality of the client or lead to a narrow preoccupation with the presenting problems. It is only one aspect of the dignostic process. It is one that is frequently neglected, however, and to the detriment of assessing the significant factors in a given situation.

If the client is a problem drinker, for example, it makes a considerable difference whether heavy drinking started in the teens or only since his wife went to a tuberculosis sanitarium eight months ago. If the former, referral for psychiatric care must be considered; if the latter, the drinking may be largely "reactive" to situational circumstances, and supportive counseling the therapy of choice. The young woman mentioned earlier is another case in point. With her, becoming engaged apparently precipitated her current maladjustment. Yet, her parents' instability suggested earlier and more pervasive problems than those for which she came for help. The diagnostic task therefore includes sorting the problems out and evaluating their significance.

The matter of *precipitating events* must also be considered here. Each of us reacts in characteristic ways to life's stressful events, and sometimes such events mark the beginning of problems that require professional help. It has been said that everyone has his breaking point, but it is equally true that people vary considerably as to what is a serious source of stress. In the combat breakdowns of World War II, for example, it appeared to be largely an individual vulnerability that determined whether the loss of a buddy, the death of a superior, the terror of a suicide attack, abandonment by the withdrawal of one's own forces, or some other drastic stimulus-situation was sufficient to overwhelm the ego defenses and produce symptoms of disintegration.

Sources of stress in ordinary life may be those of normal development from one phase of adjustment to another or they may be those of external pressures. The two sets of forces are constantly interacting, of course, and it is difficult to separate them. Crucial developmental stages and experiences include weaning, toilet training, starting school, puberty, leaving home to work or marry, and the menopause. Somewhat more "external" traumatic events include the birth of siblings, hospitalization, loss of parents during childhood or, at any age, the death of anyone of importance in one's life. Internal problems are conspicuous in such experiences, for example, as when *good* happenings are followed by *bad* reactions; such as a woman moving into a new home, long wished and planned for, only to become deeply depressed. It is therefore important to seek out and evaluate the precipitating events, if possible, and from them to form diagnostic conclusions as to whether the client's reactions are appropriate, excessive, or paradoxical, and to estimate to what extent the problems he presents are *situational, reactive*, or for the most part intrapsychic.

E. *The Nature of the Conflicts*

What has just been said about situational and other problems has to do with the nature of the conflicts. These are never absolute distinctions; they are relative, a matter of proportionate ingredients. The conflicts in a depressive reaction during the first few months of pregnancy can be differentiated from those that develop after moving into a new home. Both of these can be differentiated, in turn, from a depression that develops without any discernable external precipitating event. The total personality of the client is the important factor in all depressive reactions. The vulnerability of the individual ego to internal versus external sources of stress differs, however, just as the relative impact of external factors likewise differs from person to person.

It is for such reasons that one gauges the relative strengths and weaknesses of the person, as well as the severity of the external forces impinging upon him at the time his problems develop. A previously stable person who develops symptoms at a time of unemployment and family dissension is more vulnerable than someone who can withstand such pressures successfully. At the same time, these are *situational* problems for such persons because the chances are that they will regain their previous stability as the environmental pressures diminish. Likewise, a man who takes to drink when his wife is dying of cancer is considered to have a *reactive* problem in the sense that he is reacting in a way that, for him, is exceptional and unusual behavior, called forth only by this harrowing and tragic circumstance. Quite different is the predominantly intrapsychic conflict of the girl whose life situation is generally satisfactory, but who cannot continue on in college because she was not bid by the sorority of her choice; or the boy who contemplates suicide because he was the first in his family not to make Phi Beta Kappa. These individuals are reacting to something, certainly, but according to ordinary standards the trauma is minimal and the reaction excessive and, therefore, the problem is more within the person than in the situation.

Social workers use the concept of psychosocial diagnosis. This is closely related to what we consider here. Is the problem mostly psychological, largely social-environmental, or about fifty-fifty? We seldom know as much as we should like to know, but we must form some judgment as to the relative importance of these factors, in order to decide upon some sort of priorities in the early interviews, and to make plans for other diagnostic steps to be considered in future interviews.

F. *Medical Aspects*

A counselor, unless he is a physician, is seldom in a position to make a medical diagnosis, but he must never forget that one needs to be made. Remember, too, that "good health except for bilateral flatfoot" is a medical diagnosis, and that even such innocuous pathology can contribute to a picture of "neurasthenia" in a department store clerk. The small exceptions can be important for the counselor to evaluate.

This is more true now that so many things are considered *psychosomatic*. Clients may brush off symptoms as "psychosomatic" as a defense, because they are afraid to find out just what *is* wrong. Just as physical illnesses can mask emotional problems, so an apparent emotional illness may cover up something organic. One does not preclude the other, of course, and it is often, again, a matter of determining the relative importance of several factors. In any case, a "psychosomatic" stomach ulcer calls for medical management as much as any other kind of ulcer, even if one is also working on the psyche.

Doctors need to be reminded to consider the total personality just as much as do members of other professions. It is all too easy to fall into the either-or kind of diagnostic thinking. In *Man Against Himself*, Karl Menninger described "polysurgical addiction" in persons who, for neurotic reasons, convince surgeon after surgeon that successive operations are needed. Another type of patient, however, is able to trick physicians into the belief that their nervousness is the whole story. Counselors of all professions would do well to make sure that there is complete objective evidence for the state of a client's physical health before committing themselves to extended counseling for what appear to be—and may well be—other problems.

At a cocktail party a lady ophthalmologist raised hob with a psychiatrist because another psychiatrist treated a child for a behavior problem without prior physical examination. She, during a routine eye examination, found evidence of increased intracranial pressure. The child, alas, had a brain tumor.

A child, seen in a psychiatric clinic after stealing candy, was found to have diabetes. He felt, rightly, deprived of candy, but could not believe that it made him sick. Such cases can be multiplied. Our entirely justified preoccupation with child guidance where there are emotional difficulties must never blind us, however, to the fact that problem children may have low intelligence, be hard-of-hearing, have difficulty seeing the blackboard, be undernourished, or be physically sick in some other way. One set of conditions may influence the other, in one or both directions.

A young sailor, complaining of constant headache, was accused of malingering until he suddenly died of intracranial hemorrhage. A Navy ensign, after combat duty, developed symptoms of conversion hysteria when reassigned to another combat zone. He, too, was suspect until definite neurological signs appeared. He had a malignant tumor of the brainstem.

Adolescent girls who are upset and afraid that they are "different" because the onset of menstruation is delayed may benefit greatly from counseling. If possible, they should consult an endocrinologist as well. Adequate medical diagnosis and treatment where indicated can make the period of counseling very brief. In similar fashion, knowledge of the potentialities, as well as the limitations of the physically handicapped, frequently enhances the effectiveness of counseling.

The case of a small-town banker was dramatic but most instructive. A leader in his community and a pillar of his church, he underwent a personality change that left his family and friends aghast. Over a period of four or five weeks he became untidy, unwashed, profane, licentious, and confused. When hospitalized he was considered "schizophrenic, paranoid type" until physical examination revealed moderate heart failure. Appropriate cardiac medication and other therapy restored him in a matter of weeks and the schizophrenic reaction disappeared without a trace.

The moral is this: A physician is frequently essential to the total diagnostic process. He will sometimes establish the presence of relevant physical illness or disease. Sometimes, on the contrary, he will exclude such factors. Periodic physical examinations during long-term counseling are an additional safeguard for clients and counselors alike.

G. *A Longer Case*

A very distraught man came for marriage counseling. He was twenty-eight, his wife twenty-one, and their only child two-and-a-half. Some troubles arose from his being unemployed, others commenced earlier soon after the baby was born. Both he and his wife, as it soon appeared, came from humble backgrounds, knew little emotional security as children, and felt dominated and harshly treated by their mothers.

The client was soon diverted, however, into a detailed story of an accident some six or seven years earlier. He was driving the car, skidded on gravel and, as he felt, killed his mother who was in the car. He felt accused of doing this deliberately. His driver's license had been taken from him and he had "spent thousands" trying to get it back. He sometimes had "blackouts," he said, but he denied having epilepsy. He had never been able to talk about all this to anyone, he said.

When the wife was seen she said flatly that Mr. K. did have epilepsy and was under treatment for it. He talked constantly about the accident, she said, and was so volatile and sometimes so violent that she often feared for her life. She made some reference to some "thoughts of suicide," but it was not clear that she had made an actual attempt. A visiting nurse who had assisted Mrs. K. with infant care described Mr. K. as hostile, obnoxious, and unpopular in the neighborhood. She confirmed the epilepsy and wondered if Mr. K. was also paranoid.

The counselor responded strongly and positively to both Mr. and Mrs. K. She recognized great pent-up hostility in both. K.'s attempt to discuss the marriage was largely unsuccessful because he canceled appointments, dissected Mrs. K., and reacted to her threats of divorce. Mrs. K., on her part, complained of Mr. K.'s being unemployed and underfoot until he got a job, after which she picked up on other issues and became more agitated herself. The counselor did what she could to decrease the burden of repressed hostility of both her clients. What baffled her, however, were the reasons for Mr. K.'s at times uncontrolled behavior and the fact that with Mrs. K. "things seemed to be getting worse when externally they were better."

The consultant admired the sensitivity of the counselor's psychosocial diagnostic formulations and the skill of her attempts at marriage counseling. It seemed to him, however, that three main areas remained less than satisfactorily explored: one, the full onset and course of the epilepsy and its emotional repercussions for Mr. K.; two, the current organic status of the epilepsy; and three, the prehistory of the marriage, and its implications for the marital difficulties themselves.

The counselor had been distracted by Mr. K.'s denial of his epilepsy. When it was learned that the first attacks followed a head injury in early adolescence, a more definitive diagnosis of the epilepsy was clearly indicated. The counselor should have explored with Mr. K. his feelings and attitudes about growing up with such a frightening disability—frightening to him, to members of his family, and to anyone witnessing a seizure. At the same time the counselor should have taken steps to learn whether brain damage from the head injury was such as to preclude normal ego defenses and controls and might therefore help to explain the violent temper as well as the seizures. The fact that K. lied about his epilepsy should have alerted the counselor, but it diverted her instead.

Mrs. K. revealed that there had been no courtship prior to marriage. The two of them became "pen pals" when she was fourteen. They corresponded for nearly seven years and then married after four weeks' actual acquaintance. She had run away from home at eighteen or so, had a succession of difficult jobs at very low wages, and was almost literally grasping at a straw. What they principally had in common was a seven-year accumulation of grievances against their respective mothers and fantasies of how life might be together.

The fact that the initial request was for marriage

counseling made that, correctly, the original topic of the interview. The ensuing turmoil interfered with further diagnostic work. The counselor had little time to ask: "How did these people ever get together in the first place and what kind of marriage is it?" Nor did she complete the somatic (brain injury, epilepsy) part of the total psycho-socio-biological constellation. In many situations a limited focus, on the marriage, would have been fruitful; this was a distressing exception.

H. *Summary of the Diagnostic Process*

It is of practical importance to have a comprehensive and integrated theory of human personality. Psychoanalytic psychology, as we have seen, is one of the basic components of such a theory. The total picture of any human behavior must take into account what we arbitrarily separate into psycho-socio-biological elements. The case that has just been presented illustrates the need for such a point of view. For diagnostic understanding, the counselor needed to estimate the relative significance, not merely of psychological, social, and somatic factors in the marital interaction of the K.'s at the time they came for counseling and in prior weeks and months but, also, for purposes of prognosis and treatment planning, to discover more about the premarital development of each in all of these three spheres—physical, emotional, and social.

E. H. Erikson also speaks of three processes: the somatic process, the ego process, and the societal process. He recognizes emphatically that they are simply three ways of viewing one process, human life. In his words, this is the theory of human personality upon which a diagnosis rests:

. . . We study individual human crises by becoming

therapeutically involved in them. In doing so, we find that the three processes mentioned are three aspects of one process—i.e., human life, both words being equally emphasized. Somatic tension, individual anxiety, and group panic, then, are only different ways in which human anxiety presents itself to different methods of investigation. Clinical training should include all three methods . . .[1]

Matthew Arnold strove "to see life steadily, and see it whole." Karl Menninger speaks of a psycho-socio-physio-chemical point of view. He, Erikson, and many others have the same objective. It is a unitary or holistic view of human personality in, and in relation to, its human and material environment.

The diagnostic process must take account of all discernable elements. It is an ongoing and deepening process. It begins with a glance at the face sheet. The age of the client, the educational level, the religion—any one or all of these have their social, psychological, and biological implications. A process of "ruling in" or "ruling out" aspects of all of these elements continues during the first five minutes of the initial interview and for the duration of one's relationship with the client. There is, by the way, a whole book on "the first five minutes." It is a beautiful study not only of how much can be learned in so short a period of time but also of what we have just been discussing; namely, that a totality of personalities is involved in even so brief an encounter.[2]

Erikson's statement of the diagnostic process is as follows:

The relevance of any given item in a case history is derived from the relevance of other items to which it contributes relevance and from which, by the very fact of this contribution, it derives additional meaning. To understand a given case of psychopathology you proceed to study whatever set of observable changes seem most accessible either because they dominate the symptom presented or because you have learned a methodological approach to this particular set of items, be they the somatic changes, the personality transformations, or the social upheavals involved. Wherever you begin, you will have to begin again twice over. If you begin with the organism, it will be necessary to see what meanings these changes have in the other processes and how aggravating these meanings, in turn, are for the organism's attempt at restoration. To really understand this it will be necessary, without fear of undue duplication, to take a fresh look at the data and begin, say, with variations in the ego process, relating each item to the developmental stage and the state of the organism, as well as to the history of the patient's social associations. This, in turn, necessitates a third form of reconstruction—namely, that of the patient's family history and of those changes in his social life which receive meaning from and give meaning to his bodily changes as well as to his ego development. In other words, being unable to arrive at any simple sequence and causal chain with a clear location and a circumscribed beginning, only triple bookkeeping (or, if you wish, a systematic going around in circles) can gradually clarify the relevances and the relativities of all the known data.[3]

Karl Menninger's book, *The Vital Balance*, should be a boon to counselors. He makes a heroic effort to get away from the esoteric and often frightening diagnostic terminology of traditional writings on psychopathology. Health and sickness are relative terms. Both are expressed in terms of a vital balance, an integration of processes within the organism, and adaptation to the external environment. The organism's usual steady-state is subject to constant pressures that produce stress and give rise to tensions (discomfort, anxiety, for example) but normal coping mechanisms restore the balance. If the imbalance or upset is not severe and does not persist long we regard it as "within normal limits" and do not think in terms of sickness or serious maladjustment.

Maladjustment, sickness, emotional upset, or mental illness are described by Menninger as departures from an optimum balance, mostly as degrees of dysfunction or dyscontrol, and as the attempted substitution of another vital balance. He describes five levels of "adaptive retreat," and he holds the dynamic view of symptoms as expressions of both partial disintegration and attempted reintegration. And so-called sickness, maladjustment, or mental illness is the best adjustment that the person concerned can make at the time, given all the existing circumstances.

George L. Engel, reviewing *The Vital Balance*, puts it this way:

Health and illness then become relative terms indicating success or failure in the efforts to maintain the "vital balance." Accordingly, the terms may be as appropriately applied to disturbances or failures which are manifest in psychological or psychosocial terms (as applied to the individual) as they may be to those expressed in anatomical, physiological, or biochemical terms. Menninger, according to this view, sees mental illnesses as examples of dyscontrol or dysorganization under the impact of stress and describes recovery in terms of reorganization and recontrol. Thus, the terms "mental," "psychological," "emotional," "physical," and "organic" as applied to "disease" or "illness" serve to emphasize which systems are most deranged rather than to distinguish different states.[4]

It follows that all possibly relevant data must be considered in evaluation. This spells out the "triple bookkeeping" remark of Erikson. Menninger's "Outline for a Summary of Psychiatric Case Study Findings" is a model for any diagnostic evaluation. It is given here to suggest to counselors what should be known about a client with more than the most superficial problems. Note that the clinical data are indicated by only three words: Historical, Examinational, and Observational. This is deceptive simplicity. These words imply everything that Erikson considers essential in his previously cited passage.

I. Administrative Data (the patient's file number, age, sex, nationality, ethnic group, marital status, occupation, religious affiliation, place of normal residence, referring physician, and so forth)

II. Clinical Data
   A. Historical data
   B. Examinational data
   C. Observational data

III. Diagnostic Conclusions
   A. Appraisal of the patient's environment
      1. General features, such as geographic, climatic, national, linguistic, economic, and social
      2. Immediate features, such as family, neighborhood, work, school, church, union
      3. Particular and significant sources of support and help to the patient, and special

burdens, injuries, harassments, and over-
stimulation
4. Injuries and hardships inflicted upon the
environment by the patient
B. Appraisal of the patient
1. Somatic structure, functions, and reactions
a. Special assets (physical, psychological,
neurological)
b. Impairments (use standard nomencla-
ture and give date)
2. Psychological structure, functions, and reactions
a. Assets and potentialities (sublimations,
talents, intelligence)
b. Impairments and liabilities
(1) Preclinical (predisposition, personality disorder)
(2) Present dysorganization
(a) Degree (mild, moderate, severe)
(b) Type (acute, chronic, episodic,
recurrent)
(c) Trend (increasing, decreasing,
slow, fast)
(d) Syndrome (most nearly appropriate APA designations)
(e) Symptoms and signs
C. Explanatory formulation of the case—including the illness—on a genetic, developmental, or
dynamic basis

IV. Prognostic Conclusions
A. Probabilities regarding the further trend of the
dysorganization with or without therapeutic

intervention (listing, if helpful, the determining forces pro and con)

B. Accessibility of the patient to treatment (motivation, cooperation, economics, geography, etc.)

C. Possibilities of changing the environment in a favorable direction

Menninger's "Outline" is in his book, *The Vital Balance*.[5] For present purposes most counselors can substitute "client" for "patient." In addition, the following sections might be added:

V. Areas Requiring Further Data or Exploration With Client: Make checklist

VI. Treatment Plan or Plans:
   A. Referral
   B. Collaborative
   C. Counseling (indicate proposed techniques and goals)
      1. Supportive relationship
      2. Environmental manipulation
      3. Clarification of current reality situation and interpersonal relationships
      4. Interpretation-insight
      5. Combination
      6. Other

The treatment plan is, of course, subject to modification as the problem-solving process goes well or poorly. A preliminary treatment plan is simply an outline of the principal strategies that appear to be indicated and possible as seen from the points of view of the diagnosis and the available treatment resources.

I. *Some Diagnostic Rules of Thumb*

Few rules are absolute. The following are likely possibilities. It is a rule of thumb to consider the most common things first, but not to the exclusion of thinking of others. A person with a cough probably has a cold, but he *may* have pneumonia or cancer of a lung. A young woman with a tumor of the abdomen is pregnant until proved otherwise. The following ideas are likewise pregnant until proved otherwise:

1. Problems related to a marked personality change coming unexpectedly and rapidly indicate undiagnosed organic disease unless there are obvious external reasons such as death in the family, loss of a job, destruction of home by fire, or something comparable.

2. Problems going back a few weeks, months, or even years, coming on more gradually and appearing less out of character for the client, may be related to such critical life experiences as the birth of a sibling, move to a new home, starting school, leaving home, marriage, the menopause, retirement, etc. Careful attention to the onset and course of a client's problem will usually establish the probable connections.

3. Problems that begin early in life and persist unchanged or become worse are more difficult to treat than those more obviously related to more

recent or current inner or outer stresses. Differences in problem drinking have been mentioned. Likewise, bedwetting that has continued from infancy is generally more difficult to treat in a child of five or six than is bedwetting that stopped, and then started again after the birth of a sibling.

4. In marital problems the complaints of one spouse can usually be matched by those of the other. The responsibility is fifty-fifty. Whatever the one says about the other applies equally to himself in one fashion or another, at least in terms of unconscious impulse or wish. Most people need and want the marriages they make. The needs may be neurotic, but they generally satisfy something in both partners.

5. Problems that begin right after marriage are frequently due to sexual maladjustment. Many of these will solve themselves and others will respond to counseling. Psychoanalysis is indicated for sexual difficulties arising from neurotic conflicts, neurotic inhibitions, or related personality problems.

6. Marital problems that develop after the birth of the first or second child are (in the absence of economic hardship) commonly due to the frustrated, passive, dependent strivings of both partners.

7. It is important to know whether one is dealing with the first or the fifteenth episode of certain problems since this has implications for the degree of severity and for treatability. One divorce may indicate an immaturity now past. Three divorces

suggest persistent neurotic or other personality problems. The same holds for loss of jobs, stealing, school failures, and many other problems of personal adjustment.

8. The client who comes under duress will remain only under duress. There are notable exceptions and there are special techniques for working in an "authoritative setting." Generally speaking, however, a person has to want help in order to accept it.

9. The phenomena of the first interview can be very deceptive. Some clients are markedly less hostile, suspicious, anxious, or withdrawn by the second appointment. Others, with good facades and projective defenses, reveal the full extent of their pathology only in later interviews.

10. The social history is a tissue of lies and is therefore useless. The social history is an invaluable tool for the understanding of a client's personality and adaptive capacities and for an evaluation of his problems in the context of his family and larger environment. Both statements are true!

The counselor must learn what he can as he goes along. He gives the client free rein to reveal himself, but he does not hesitate to ask questions in order to fill in gaps or get specific answers about crucial matters. The counselor must expect the defensive operations of the ego to produce denials, distortions, and total repression of some data whether he is talking with a client or others close to him. Any formulation, like any interpretation, is valid for the day and in the context of the available material. It is therefore subject to revision at any time.

Here are some practical suggestions for getting diagnostic leads quickly. Again, they are guidelines, not universal laws:

1. Study the face sheet for diagnostic clues:
   a. The name may indicate an ethnic group or a marriage involving two ethnic groups and therefore the possibility of typical problems.
   b. The age narrows the range of likely problems.
   c. Marital status both suggests and excludes possibilities.
   d. Educational level says something about intelligence, adaptive opportunities, and potential ego strengths.
   e. Religious affiliation may have cultural implications and suggest typical problems.
   f. The number of children, if any, the timing of their arrival with respect to the date of marriage and to each other may speak volumes.
   g. The sex of the client, the occupation, the income level and comparable details, if available, are of importance in gauging adaptive capacities and likely problem areas.

2. Note the client's appearance:
   a. Well-groomed, quite apart from matters of taste and income, means intact ego. Quite sick, particularly depressed, clients are likely to neglect their grooming or to present an inappropriate, sometimes bizarre appearance. Schizophrenic clients can be a notable exception.

b. Facial expression is patently important; also, gait, response to conventional greeting, moist palm, and other such details.

c. Reread *The Adventures of Sherlock Holmes* as a reminder!

3. Take note of your subjective responses to the client, but remember that these may tell as much about you as about the client:

a. You may like or dislike, feel protective, find appealing, be sexually interested, be offended, feel perplexed. There are many possibilities. What about the client has aroused such responses? How much is his problem, how much yours?

(1) A strikingly or flashily dressed individual is often very narcissistic, wanting the attention of all eyes, and this may indicate unusual passive, dependent demands or wishes.

(2) A seductive male (granting cultural differences) is insecure, strongly homoerotic, or searching for an ideal mother, if not all three together.

(3) A seductive female is insecure, sexually maladjusted (frigid or deprived or both), and also searching for an ideal mother.

(4) The hostile, aggravating client is very anxious, probably "testing" and generally wanting acceptance very much.

b. If you do not like the client or like him too much, you had better refer him to someone else. Unless you have time for a personal psychoanalysis, you do not need to know why. If this is a problem with many clients, however, you should consider a personal analysis. The same holds if you overprotect, withdraw, get upset, or are otherwise uncomfortable in the relationship. You do not have to decide during the first interview, of course, but you should before there is a "treatment compact" for continuing counseling.

4. Get a medical history:
   a. Not in the first five minutes, but do not neglect it. This protects everyone.
   b. Even the "usual" childhood illnesses may have had more serious complications; e.g., encephalitis.
   c. Childhood illnesses and operations, especially with hospitalization, are part of a psychosocial as well as medical history because such experiences and related fantasies breed feelings of inferiority, punishment, and rejection.
   d. Recent medical contacts are important; it is important to know whether clients are on medications, and if these are being supervised.
   e. If the client has not had a recent physical examination he should be advised and helped to do so. Summer camps, colleges, graduate schools of social work, etc., require them as a routine precaution. So should counselors. A childhood behavior problem such as stealing may be caused or influenced by feeblemindedness, diabetes, a need to provoke punishment, epilepsy, a broken home, a vitamin deficiency, a wish to belong to a group or other psycho-socio-biological factors. It takes a physician to help evaluate some of these.

5. Consider consultation or referral early:
   a. Consultation enables you to complete your diag-

nostic task whether it is with a colleague, supervisor, social worker, doctor, psychologist, clinic, or psychiatrist.

b. It is generally easier to tell the client firmly, "This is necessary," during the diagnostic phase than later, after hours of interviewing.

c. Early consultation is not an act of desperation or admission of defeat.

d. In all but really routine and superficial matters, it may save someone—client, counselor, agency, or community—countless hours and countless dollars, if one comes to grips early with the diagnostic problem.

1. Erik H. Erikson, *Childhood and Society*, 2nd ed. (New York: W. W. Norton & Co., 1963), p. 37.

2. Robert E. Pittenger, Charles F. Hockett, and John J. Danehy, *The First Five Minutes* (Ithaca, New York: Paul Martineau, 1960).

3. Erikson, pp. 45–46.

4. George L. Engel, "Mental Illness: Vital Balance or Myth?" *Bulletin of the Menninger Clinic*, 28:145–153, 1964.

5. Karl Menninger, *The Vital Balance* (New York: The Viking Press, 1963), pp. 330–331.

CHAPTER FOUR

To Keep or to Refer the Client?

One of the purposes of the first interview—or the first few interviews—is for the counselor and the client to determine whether they can and should work together. The fact that both diagnostic and therapeutic processes are part of even the first meeting between counselor and client does not alter the fact that this first meeting may be the last. One part of the diagnostic problem is whether there is to be a continuing relationship or whether the client should seek other help. In the one instance, there will be an agreement or understanding about working together; in the other, a carefully considered referral to someone else.

A. *The Decision*

As the client's story unfolds, the counselor begins thinking about the problem of focus. The question is not simply whether the client is in the right place considering *the* problem, but whether he is in the right place considering the *aspect* of the problem that requires first attention or can be most usefully dealt with. The decision is sometimes very simple: The client reveals difficulties that are beyond the counselor's competence or are outside the agency's functions, if the counselor works in an agency. The decision to refer can therefore be made at once. At other times, however, much has to be sorted out before the decision can be made.

Counselors sometimes find it difficult to accept the limits of the time available or of the agency in which they work. This is a problem that they must resolve for their own peace of mind and for the welfare of their clients. School counselors, workers in public agencies, and others are frequently tempted to bootleg treatment services outside their agency programs. Their motives are praiseworthy, perhaps, but they unwittingly put the client in the position of being trapped between authorities in conflict. The analogy of one parent enlisting the sympathies of a child against the other parent is partly apt even though the client is not a child. Careful studies have shown that psychiatric hospital patients get worse when the doctor and nurse are at odds, and this analogy, too, is partly apropos. On the whole, it is better for the counselor to accept the limitations of the agency *in his dealings with clients,* and to express elsewhere any feelings about its shortcomings.

One "hard core" public assistance family is a case in point. Seven members of this particular family had for years known sickness, school problems, vocational maladjustment, and unemployment. They required public assistance and aid to dependent children. Their caseworker was unable to help them use their money efficiently, however, and apparently encouraged them to feel that they were not getting enough. Perhaps this was so, but they were getting what the law allowed.

In the course of time, the several members of the

family submerged their individual problems in a sort of group paranoia directed against the public agency. The family got along famously. Their only problem, it now appeared, was that they "didn't get enough relief." The worker, who felt this herself, was stymied.

A new worker, however, was able to cut through this irrational adjustment. She was quite firm about the limitations of the agency, and pointed out that the family failed to use efficiently what funds there were. With skillful, reality-oriented counseling, this worker helped the older members of the family onto the road to independence and the younger ones to a better school adjustment. Important individual problems certainly remained, but the group paranoia was dispelled and a host of family needs provided for effectively.

The problem of focus, then, is partly a matter of the client's needs, partly a matter of the counselor's training, and partly—if an agency is involved—a matter of that agency's function. Suppose the clients are prospective adoptive parents who will be refused a child. The worker is perfectly competent to counsel with this couple about the reasons for the agency's refusal and all of their feelings about it. If agency policy is against such counseling, however, the worker can only drop the matter (knowing the need) or refer the couple to other private or community counseling resources.

Some necessary decisions do not present themselves transparently. A young mother once came for help because her five-year-old son could not fall asleep at night. It took a home visit to reveal the fact that the mother's bedtime kiss, full on the lips, was for a lover and not for a son of any age. The immediate treatment was obvious and the benefits equally so, but the long-range treatment involved the marriage and included the mother's psychoanalysis. A child's problem is frequently the mother's problem or the parents' problem, but it should never be forgotten that a child, past infancy, is quite capable of having conflicts of his own. The growing child soon comes to see the world through his own eyes and to react to it with the uniqueness of his own personality structures; he cannot be understood, therefore, entirely in terms of reactions to or identifications with his parents. A counselor can often be very helpful in changing detrimental patterns of interaction between parents, or between parents and children. When the parents or the children cannot change, however, because of unconscious inner conflicts, then psychoanalysis may be the treatment of choice.

Sometimes the counselor has to settle for limited goals. This word *limited* has a ring of failure to it, but one should avoid this feeling. Counseling, like diplomacy, is always the art of the possible.

Suppose the client is a chronic "loner," say an ambulatory schizophrenic. His greatest need, perhaps, is to simply "check in" with someone once or twice a month. This will not cure him, but it may well sustain him. Such a client will often make clear the extent of his need, and to offer more can be a mistake.

There are many situations in which the counselor will do well to say, "Let's see how much we can accomplish in six interviews." This can work miracles. Six interviews are enough in which to separate out environmental factors from firmly rooted inner conflicts or personality traits. They allow enough time for mobilization of what ego strengths there are. Careful delineation of problem areas may well suffice to allow the client to come to grips with those things that he can do something about, and to put aside those things about which nothing can fruitfully be done.

Unless there are clear indications for long-term counseling—and the indications include the counselor's training as well as the client's need—there is much to be said for a limited number of appointments. There are many "dropouts" after a few sessions anyway, and there might be fewer if a limit was set in advance. It is sad but true, moreover, that many people work best against a deadline. Limited numbers of appointments help to avoid the magical expectations and related dependency problems that so often arise in long-term therapy. These are most difficult to work with even when unconscious strivings and demands can be interpreted in the relationship.

Counselors, in common with other therapists, have to think actively about the treatment or treatments of choice considering the client's problems and his total situation. If environmental pressures are the principal reason for the client's presenting problems, then the first order of business is to do what can be done about reducing those pressures. The counselor may well continue working with the client, but at the same time call upon other professional or community resources for various kinds of assistance. If, by contrast, the problems arise primarily from intrapsychic conflicts of long standing, the counselor will have to consider referral to a psychoanalyst or other psychiatrist. The common assumption that the client cannot afford such services is sometimes arrived at too easily. Much depends upon the flexibility of fee scales as well as the presence of clinics and similar resources.

Most of life's problems arise, to be sure, from a combination of pressures. Nevertheless we see and describe them as predominantly environmental, interpersonal, intrapsychic, or somatic. In any case, as we have seen, some 70 per cent of clients with problems will turn initially to clergymen or family physicians for help. These counselors have, therefore, a unique opportunity and responsibility to sort out the significant causative factors in a given problem situation. It is they who must decide when to call upon others for diagnostic help or more definitive treatment services.

B. *The Agreement to Work Together*

When the counselor decides that he can offer service to the client, it is up to him to say so and to clarify with the client what can or cannot be expected and how the two will go about the process. In one fashion or another the counselor says, "I think that we can usefully work together on your problems, and here is how we can go about it." The principal dangers are two: (1) the counselor's assumption that the client has a realistic knowledge of the ways and limitations of counseling; and (2) the client's assumption that the counselor has every resource it takes to solve the problems at hand.

Speaking of psychoanalysis, Franz Alexander once said that a patient should have at least an *intellectual* knowledge of the procedure and its rationale, plus at least a skeptical willingness to give it a try before he is put on the couch and asked to associate freely. In principle, this is true for counseling. Clients have the right to ask how this will help, and to be told that it may not help; or that, in any case, it will not solve everything. Some will not believe this, even if told—such being the power of hope and faith—but they need to be told anyway because a part of them will hear it.

It is important to clarify early whatever limitations there will be. If the limitations are those of agency function, they must be spelled out. The same is true so far as the counselor's time, training, and special interests are concerned. The agency can or cannot give financial assistance. This will have to be explained at once to certain clients. The counselor will or will not see other members of a family. The interviews are strictly confidential or they are not. This matter is often of the highest importance when one is dealing with children or when the client, of any age, is responsible to some civil or other authority. One should never imply, make, or permit to be inferred any commitment that cannot be fulfilled.

Clarity about the formal arrangements is equally important: if there is to be a fee, if there are to be regular appointments, if the counselor is shortly to take a vacation, or if there will be a change of counselors. If these or other matters enter into the agreement to work together they, too, should be spelled out in advance. This is not to suggest, of course, that business matters have to be disposed of in a first interview if the client is in some acute distress. The point is, rather, that they should be out of the way and understood at about the time the preliminary diagnostic phase is over and the counselor is ready to suggest a number of problem-solving interviews, whether six, sixty, or, as it may turn out, one hundred and sixty!

The reason for understanding now is to avoid misunderstanding later. The counselor and the client will both be too busy with other matters to become embroiled in questions of "Why didn't you explain this to me at the beginning?" If the counseling takes the form of extended therapy, the client's transference reactions (see following) will be more clearly and effectively dealt with if the relationship, in its formal aspects, is realistically and clearly defined at the outset. Life has enough ambiguities without unnecessary ones, and straightforward arrangements are therefore indicated at the outset regarding what fee is reasonable, what appointment times are possible, and what policies are to obtain about missed appointments, vacations, and related matters.

The inadequacies of language as an instrument of communication are well known but often forgotten. A young man once gave a long and philosophical dissertation on this subject to a young woman friend. She ended up with hurt feelings and the conviction that all he was saying was that he could not understand her. Unconsciously she was probably right, but that was not what he intended to say!

In counseling, communication is doubly difficult because of the fears, shame, guilt, and at the same time magical expectations, that the client usually brings to the interviews. What the client hears may be wish-fulfilling. He may take as criticism what the counselor intends to be an objective question or confrontation. The anxious client is in part a frightened child, and the words of the counselor may be heard with the ears of a frightened child.

Educational, cultural, linguistic, and other differences between counselor and client may complicate communication further. As political campaigns sometimes demonstrate, words do not have the same meanings for the educated and the uneducated. It is still possible to have a gay time at a party in Iowa, but "gay" in San Francisco connotes homosexuality. And as for adolescents, one is fortunate to be able to communicate with them in any language!

During World War II, a young man was sent home from boot camp. A psychiatrist, wishing to soften the blow of a discharge for psychiatric reasons, wrote to the parents that the boy had "personality difficulties" that precluded successful adaptation to Navy life. Almost by return mail the mother wrote back outraged; she wanted the Navy to know that her son had a *wonderful personality* and she intended to write to her congressman about this affront to the family honor.

Medical social work came into being partly because of such problems of communication. The story is told of the famous Dr. Richard Clarke Cabot that he sent a cardiac patient home with instructions to rest. He subsequently discovered that the patient interpreted "rest" to mean lying on a couch near the telephone and making dozens of calls in an effort to raise money for a favorite charity. It was at this point, the story goes, that Dr. Cabot realized the importance of the counseling interview in which the doctor's recommendations could be discussed and rediscussed in detail until the patient understood in concrete terms the implications of "rest," for example, as applied to climbing stairs, getting meals, staying in bed, having visitors, and a host of related matters.

Another patient was ordered to rest following cardiac surgery. Some months later she was seen by a psychiatrist because of vague symptoms that her internist could not account for. It soon appeared that there was a marital problem and that this was due, in part, to the fact that the couple was not having sexual intercourse. The husband had interpreted "rest" to mean "no excitement" whatsoever, and had therefore, without explanation, avoided his wife sexually. Lack of communication between husband and wife compounded the problem of lack of communication between doctor and patient, but the situation improved considerably when this couple found out that sexual intercourse was not taboo because of the operation.

Communication in counseling, then, takes time, patience, and awareness of sources of confusion and misunderstanding. Such awareness is important during the initial interview, at the time of making arrangements for continued counseling, or when the necessity arises for referring the client to some other person or agency. This is still another

reason why the professional attitude protects both counselor and client and why "being friendly" can be disastrous.
The humorous remark, the "light touch," the revelation of
one's own feelings and attitudes are too often taken by the
client as meaning "he doesn't understand," "he doesn't take
me seriously," "he isn't listening to *my* problems," or "he
must think this is a cocktail party." Not that everything
must be in deadly earnest, of course; it is a matter of tact
and timing. The point is that a good bedside manner and its
equivalents in counseling are no substitute for a quick grasp
of the essentials of the client's situation and an empathic
response to them.

C. *Making a Referral*

The decision to refer a client to someone else is of self-
evident importance in the mind of the counselor, but not
necessarily so in the feelings of the client. The counselor
must give the client valid intellectual reasons for the referral
and then help him to arrive at an emotional acceptance as
well. The counselor must also help the client to avoid expecting too little or too much.

It is axiomatic, of course, that the counselor should know
other resources in the community. Larger cities have direc-
tories of social and welfare agencies. The 1963 *Social Service Directory of Metropolitan Chicago,* for example, runs
to more than two hundred pages. A call to the local family
agency or public health officer will sometimes do the trick.
Do you know, for example, that no matter what his age,
the feebleminded "child" of a retired worker is entitled to
social security benefits? Or that you cannot get aid for dependent children of a common-law marriage in certain
states, but that courts can legalize such marriages at their

discretion? These particular answers, oddly enough, came from syndicated newspaper columns, but they indicate the sort of problems one may have to ask about. There are clubs for women alcoholics, for parents of retarded children, for persons who have been in mental hospitals, for parents without spouses, for people in their sixties and beyond, and so on. There are groups who will make phone calls to persons who are alone, who will visit the bedridden, who will provide substitute fathers or older brothers, who will read to the blind. Some are good, some bad, and some indifferent, but they are likely to go unnoticed unless someone bothers to catalog them or unless counselors inform themselves of their existence.

A referral is, of course, a matter of matching a need and a resource. The need must be identified as the most important or, at least, as the most urgent of the client's problems. This, too, is something that the client should understand and emotionally accept. In view of the effort it has taken for the client to come for help in the first place and the inevitable resentment and feeling of rejection at being passed on to someone else, the reasons for the referral may well require repeated interpretation and emotional working through. The client even more than the counselor must come to recognize the major problem and to have a clear connection between this and the new resource to which he is being referred.

The most important reason for all of this, of course, is to ensure that the client will follow through on the referral. The counselor seldom wants to be so protective and paternalistic as to accompany the client in person, although this is sometimes precisely the thing to do. He knows, however, that there are many "dropouts" under the most favorable circumstances and he does well to remember that feelings of rejection, disappointment, and extra effort required may well become excuse enough for a dropout at this point unless the referral is skillfully handled. It is another instance of helping a client effectively to help himself.

A realistic problem for many counselors is that of extremely limited community resources. Thousands of communities are without agencies, clinics, specialized hospitals, or visiting nurses. Available counselors may be limited to busy general practitioners, clergymen, county judges, or law enforcement officers, and personnel of public welfare agencies. Psychotic patients may go to the county jail and delinquent children to the state reformatory or "correctional school." Not too many years ago, the population of a school for the mentally deficient (subject to sterilization, by the way) was found to have many children of normal or even superior intelligence who had been confined for punitive reasons. "There are times," one grass-roots social worker has said, "when all that you can do is to write your congressman."

Few cities have the right to be complacent. The selective intake policies of psychiatric clinics, for example, can send a flow of "untreatable" or "very long term treatment" clients to family agencies or other counseling services where, indeed, they frequently became "untreatable" or "very long term treatment" clients, leaving the counselors wondering if they are really prepared to deal with this type of client and whether, therefore, it is part of "agency function" to accept them for more than very limited service. Few cities have "halfway houses" for people discharged from mental hospitals and not quite ready to live alone or with their families. Not many places have separate facilities for "delinquent" children under court jurisdiction and other children, also wards of the court, who simply need a protective service pending foster home placement, placement with relatives, or other arrangements following the death, divorce, or incarceration of their parents.

Sometimes, however, the feelings of the counselor are the real obstacle to a satisfactory referral. Many of us have a *need* to help that is unreasonably beyond the limits of a *wish* to help. Such a *need* has the effect of a compulsion that carries with it the conviction that we *must* do the job or, even, that *only we* can do the job. As Julius Caesar said, ". . . such men are dangerous!"

It sometimes happens that the counselor shares certain prejudices with the client, or he may assume that the client has prejudices that are really his own. Such attitudes are seen when appropriate referral to a psychiatrist is avoided "because only crazy people go to a psychiatrist," or to a social worker "because that is asking for charity," or to a clergyman "because he will try to convert you." There is, of course, some basis for such concerns, historically if not currently; but it is more accurate to assume that counseling, in whatever setting, is increasingly becoming an objective, knowledgeable profession.

The counselor must be prepared to deal with these fears. They are part of the client's reluctance to make a change, to begin (as it feels to him) all over again. It is part of the counselor's responsibility to make it a good referral; i.e., to protect the client as much as possible against a series of referrals that may, in the end, breed discouragement and apathy. All of this requires special tact when the client has come eager for help and has his hopes up to an unrealistic degree. It will take time and emotional working through for him to understand why the counselor cannot see the problem as he sees it and why, from the counselor's point of view, the client is in the wrong place. In short, then, the counselor who refers a client to someone else must clearly and carefully define the problem; must specifically and convincingly relate the problem to the new resource; must make sure that he and the client are "talking the same language" and therefore understand each other; and must help the client to become aware of and express his feelings about the referral to the point that they are not an obstacle to its success.

CHAPTER FIVE

Some Paradoxes of Counseling

Anyone who does counseling must be prepared for unusual behavior on the part of clients. The client comes for help, and then refuses to be frank about himself. Or he becomes provocative toward the very person from whom he wants help. The counselor, on his part, finds that he gets sleepy when listening to certain clients or talks more than he knows he should or becomes more protective of the client than is really necessary. It is astonishing that such irrational behaviors can enter into even the briefest of counseling relationships.

We cannot always do much about these phenomena, but it helps to be aware of them. Sometimes they are simply the outward manifestations of anxiety, the sort of thing that one expects in initial interviews. They may, of course, represent habitual "built-in" personality defenses, persisting beyond the early interviews and being more or less characteristic of the client in all of his relationships. In any case, they vary from client to client; they are more obvious with some counselors than with others; and, to some extent, they are (with most clients) more conspicuous in longer counseling relationships than in brief contacts. We shall discuss some of these paradoxical behaviors under their technical terms: resistance, regression, transference, and counter-transference.

A. *Resistance*

The term *resistance* has several connotations. It may be conscious or unconscious; i.e., the client may or may not be aware of what he is doing. He comes for help, but is very reluctant about it. He is ambivalent, having feelings pro and feelings con. The latter are a source of resistance, and this may express itself in conscious reservations about the step he is taking or in unconscious delaying tactics, missing a bus or forgetting an appointment. Just as there is resistance to going to the dentist so there is resistance to seeing a counselor, and for comparable reasons.

The initial resistance, then, has mostly to do with feelings of shame at having to ask for help. Closely related are painful feelings about the matters to be talked about; the guilt, shame, and fear, for example, about marital infidelity or a pregnancy out of wedlock. It is asking quite a bit, after all, to get someone to tell you, no matter how many degrees you have or how professional or how kindly and understanding, the innermost secrets of his heart. He is not likely to do it except under the pressure of great necessity, and even then only after he has had a chance to feel you out and find some basis for trusting you. Remember, then, that while some clients will give a straightforward story in the first fifteen minutes, others will be devious, drop hints, ask leading questions, or beat about the bush for a long time before coming to the point—or the *real* point—of their request for help. Sometimes, of course, they have blinded themselves to the real point, and it will be part of the counseling task to bring this into conscious focus.

Resistance refers also to the reluctance to make changes

even though changes are clearly indicated. We know this from everyday life. Young children want to play the same game or be told the same story time after time and without the slightest deviation. Middle-aged and older people are "set in their ways." So are we all about cherished beliefs and well-established patterns of behavior. These, after all, are part of our habitual defensive operations; they may not be very good, but they are the best we have and it *seems* dangerous to give them up. Also, so far as most of us are concerned, there may be other unconscious gratifications in many of the very problems we complain of most bitterly.

Four department heads at a certain university had serious "heart attacks" within a period of two years. Four adults, who should know better, drove themselves that hard! Granted that others drive themselves and get away with it, the point is that so many complain of overwork and go on overworking. Sometimes it is *really* necessary, but often the gratifications (underneath the gripes) are prestige, competition, meeting parental expectations, and the like. Few such cases come to counselors, perhaps, but among those who do there will be, as we shall see, many whose most cherished complaints also contain their hidden pleasures. This being the case, the conscious wish to change or to do something about the problem will be strongly resisted by the hidden satisfactions that say, in effect, "No, I really can't let go of this."

The resistance against coming for help and the resistance to changing are not always found together. Some clients will come all too willingly, and then settle down for a ten-year tenure. The gratification is in coming, but not in changing anything. The relationship with the counselor is, for them, the solution. It is a would-be cure for loneliness, a source of support and reassurance, and, at times, a substitution of talk for necessary action. There are even a few places where this is the "thing to do" in the neighborhood. Just as the *New Yorker* could carry an advertisement, a few years ago, "Carry this handkerchief when you see your analyst," so in other areas it has status value to be able to say, "I'm going to see my social worker or my counselor." The motivations of man are many and mixed!

There are also the resistances that arise more directly from unconscious psychic operations. All of us have repressed painful childhood memories, and we continue to repress whatever threatens to arouse anxiety. Counseling usually involves *some* self-examination; sometimes a great deal. And the more this process leads us to the painful, the frightening, the shameful aspects of our secret thoughts, fantasies, motives, and behaviors, the more resistances will be aroused. The counselor's task is to anticipate this and, when appropriate, to make the client aware of it; and this in itself will often be sufficient to enable the client to overcome his resistance and to go on.

This, then, is a paradox. The client comes for help and then opposes it. The counselor, until he becomes experienced, is baffled and even angered by such behavior. The more a counselor has an emotional investment in helping people, the more frustrated and angry he will be at the client's resistance. This will only provoke more resistance, of course; and the client is likely to respond further by defeating the counselor's need to help. It has been said with much wisdom that a counselor's therapeutic ambition arouses the most profound resistances. The client, sensing that the treatment is for the therapist's narcissistic gratification, reacts with rejected fury and, unless his own need is vastly greater, destroys the therapist's efforts every time.

The counselor seldom knows directly that he is angry. He infers it, however, by its signs and symptoms. He is bored. He suppresses yawns. His attention wanders. He smokes too much. He talks too much. He becomes too helpful (overly protective). He reasons with the client, or even argues with him. His ulcers get worse or he develops a migraine. Assuming, then, that he began the appointment in fair health and spirits, the counselor should take a second look at changes in mood or muscle tension arising during the interview. These changes may point to something important in the material and in his own reactions to the client or perhaps (as will be seeen from the following) to problems within himself.

What has been said previously indicates that the client is bound to have some resistance to counseling. It has also been pointed out that expectations of the counselor may provoke other resistances. It has been suggested, finally, that signs or symptoms within the counselor himself may provide the clue to the fact that the client is resisting one or another aspect of the counselor's activity. Besides the client's resistance there are other possibilities to be considered; these include the client's regressive tendencies and transference reactions, and also the counselor's transference or countertransference responses.

B. *Regression*

Regression means reverting to behavior of an earlier developmental phase or level. A child who has been successfully toilet trained, but who resumes wetting or soiling after the birth of a younger sibling, has regressed. Or a client who becomes completely helpless in the course of counseling has regressed. Indications of regression may sometimes be seen in tone of voice, in vocabulary, in overt or subtle attitudes toward the counselor; or in various total behaviors in the home, on the job, or in the wider community.

A client may be regressed when he first comes for help.

The pressures of inner anxiety or outer causes of stress can contribute to such regressive behaviors as whining, temper tantrums, adolescent attitudes, or loss of initiative and incentive. Even if relatively mature, however, the client may display regressive tendencies through inappropriate reactions during early interviews. These may take the form of unrealistic ideas, "magical" thinking, or illogical assumptions or expectations. A very common experience of this type occurs when the client tells his story and then stops cold, as if to say: "Now it's in your lap; do something!"

When counseling extends over a period of weeks or months, regressive tendencies may be referable to the treatment itself. An accentuation of passive-dependent attitudes is the most commonly encountered. In such instances it becomes part of the counselor's task to ask himself how much of such change comes from the client and how much comes from the counselor himself. If it is the client, the explanation may be in the pressure of his problems, in a strengthening of his wishes to be taken care of, or in various transference reactions vis-à-vis the counselor. At the same time, however, the counselor may have to examine his own attitudes and activity with the question as to whether he has contributed, by overprotectiveness or other unnecessary activity, to the intensification of the client's regressive tendencies.

Robert P. Knight once wrote an article for nurses on "why patients behave the way they do in the hospital." He spoke particularly about regressive reactions, and defenses against them. People who are threatened by their (mostly unconscious) wishes to regress are likely to protest being sick. They refuse to have a back rub, they fail to stay in bed, and they fight their medications. Unconsciously wanting very much to be "nursed," they resist the nursing care that is appropriate to their illness. They comprise some of the difficult and uncooperative patients with whom nurses have to work, and their counterparts are found in counseling as well.

Then there are those who enjoy the regression. They want more nursing care than they need or are entitled to, and they become demanding, whining, and overly dependent. When the time comes, it is difficult to get them out of bed. Sometimes they are overly dependent on sedation or even become addicted to narcotics. It is easy to become angry with such patients and with clients in counseling who are like them. One has to remember that they are frightened, that regression is a reaction to anxiety. What they are now doing was once appropriate; that is, it was once normal to be a baby and to act like one. Regression is not merely a going back to an earlier developmental level; it is also a going back to adaptive patterns that once were both appropriate and successful.

When a patient "falls in love" with a doctor or a nurse, the same regressive pattern is involved. When one is sick, all feelings of the frightened, helpless child may be aroused. When danger is over, however, what is more appropriate than to love the powerful protector, the one who has "kissed it and made it well." The same principles apply to the regressive phenomena of counseling.

C. *Transference*

The importance of transference in human relationships would be hard to overestimate. Transference means attributing to another person traits, qualities, feelings, ideas, etc., which do not necessarily belong to him, but which we assume belong to him by reason of some similarity to ourselves or to others that we have known. The more usual definition of transference is that it is the *unconscious* transfer to new persons of feelings that we originally had toward the key persons of earlier life. Such a transfer of feelings, however, is predicated upon our seeing these new objects as being similar to or like the previous ones; e.g., *this* redhead (we assume) is like *that* redhead of childhood or *this* boss is like *that* father, because both exercise power and authority. In therapy, transference means the unconscious feelings, attitudes, and reactions toward the therapist as he is assumed to be in some parental, competitive, sexual, or other object role. Any irrational way of relating to another person—i.e., any thoughts, feelings, or other behavior not evoked or provoked by the other person or otherwise justified by the realities of the relationship—may be thought of as a transference. The following paragraphs will deal with several aspects of transference: definition, motivation, and manifestations.

The broadest *definition* of transference, perhaps, is to the effect that we experience the present in terms of the past. What is more commonly meant by the term, however, is that we tend to endow present-day objects with the attributes of past—particularly, childhood—objects and to repeat in current relationships the emotional and other behavioral patterns of earlier interpersonal relationships. Many authors are careful—and rightly so—to emphasize the *subjectivity* of all this; e.g., we endow our percepts or images of present objects with our "pictures," "images," or imagos —compounded of fact, fantasy, wish, fear, projection, etc.— of former objects. It goes without saying that what appears as transference is (or has been) repressed; in other words, it is unconscious, so far as a client is concerned, until it can be rendered conscious in a therapeutic situation.

Although transferences are a fact of everyday life, most discussions of them apply to the psychoanalytic or other psychotherapeutic situation. A few authors contend that all feelings, attitudes, or other behavior toward the therapist is transference, but the majority would modify this by saying that only the inappropriate, irrational components are transference. From a pragmatic point of view it is not transference, for example, if the client's response has been provoked by the counselor or if the client is reacting to the counselor "as he really is." Robert Waelder epitomizes what may be called a "standard definition":

> Transference is not simply the attribution to new objects of characteristics of old ones but the attempt to reestablish and relive, with whatever object will permit it, an infantile situation much longed for because it was once either greatly enjoyed or greatly missed.[1]

Herman Nunberg, however, does not call it transference if the client attempts to compel the therapist to be like an object of the past, but rather a "readiness for transference." [2] We must deal, therefore, with multiple definitions and connotations of the term transference.

Karl Menninger [3] pays tribute to Alfred Korzybski for insisting upon distinguishing the identity (i.e., image) of any particular person or thing by a precise statement of time, place, and circumstance. "Mother" when we are three years old, for example, is not "Mother" when we are five or seven or thirteen; nor is "Mother happy" by any means the same as "Mother angry." Just as important: "Mother" is by no means the same when *I* am gratified at age three as she is when *I* am frustrated at age three, both because I will perceive her differently (partly due to projection of my own feelings) and because I will alter my perceptions in accordance with whatever my behavior stirs up in her. Such images are experienced and then become repressed, but sometimes reappear in later life as transferences.

Here are some of the kinds or forms of transference. They may be stated in the form of a series of propositions with a brief commentary on each.

1. "I (the client) perceive you (the counselor) to be (or to be like) my father (mother, sibling, priest, etc.)." This, in essence, is the classical form of transference as a phenomenon.

2. "I (the client) demand that you (the counselor) *be* (or *become*) my father (mother, etc.)." This, according to Nunberg, is readiness for transference, but not transference; however, most authors would call it a form of transference.

3. "I (the client) demand that you (the counselor) be as my parents (or others) *ought* to have been." This attitude is characteristic of a transference neurosis when the client's demands for gratification by the counselor smother his wishes for insight and cure.

4. "I (the client) expect you (the counselor) to judge me and to reward or punish me." This illustrates projection of the client's superego; the superego comprising, of course, more or less archaic images of parents and other authorities.

5. "I (the client) knew that you (the counselor) wanted me to 'live it up' at the party." The client sets aside his own superego and perceives the counselor as being on the side of his impulses or as being more permissive than his own superego. At the same time, he shifts responsibility and avoids guilt by making the counselor the "keeper of his conscience."

6. "I (the client) demand that you (the counselor) accept me as I am—good or bad, clean or dirty, etc." This kind of transference demand is implicit in much "acting out."

7. "You (the counselor) blanched and drew away from me when I (the client) stood up to leave; you must have thought I was going to murder you." An intensification of drives has resulted in a misperception at the end of an interview, the latter indicating transference.

8. "I (the client) am just like you (the counselor); I can understand everyone around me." A defensive identification with the counselor is often a defense against transference feelings and against insight; the client "analyzes" everyone but himself!

9. "You (the counselor) love me (the client) and will take care of me, but he (husband, father, etc.) hates me and refuses to help me." The "divided" or "split" transference is suggested here. One object is loved, another hated by virtue of a separation of unconscious ambivalence toward some early object. Another example, significant for some groups, is: "We (members of this group) love and support each other, but we hate him or her or them (the scapegoat)."

The phenomena of transference, then, can be listed in terms of the displacement of images and affects onto the counselor or in terms of the revival, in the therapy, of earlier (perhaps frustrated) interpersonal relationships—or a combination of the two. Transference manifestations occur "within" the counseling situation, in "acting out" or in everyday life.

Discussion of the management of transference boils down to questions of interpretation, manipulation, or some admixture of both. Psychoanalysts, by and large, limit themselves to interpretation. Considerations of *what* to interpret —e.g., intrapsychic conflicts, maternal rejection, "faulty" identifications, and so on—vary with the theoretical orientation of the therapist, the nature of the therapy, the apparent psychopathology, and the therapeutic goals. Techniques of transference interpretation are patently one thing for a classical psychoanalyst working with a "classical" case of psychoneurosis and quite another thing for a counselor dealing with an acute marital crisis.

The literature on transference phenomena and techniques in "brief psychotherapy" or in counseling with infrequent appointments is not extensive. In the case of infrequent visits much of the transference is diluted, diffused, and displaced onto others than the therapist. There are, however, dramatic exceptions. Many therapists, we know, wish to avoid intense transference states—particularly the transference neurosis—because of the conviction that these entail too much regression and dependency and thereby impede therapeutic results, if not defeating them altogether. Important studies have yet to be made regarding the fate of transferences in counseling and in psychotherapies other than psychoanalysis.

D. *Transference and Resistance*

If one understands transference he understands much about resistance. In addition to reasons for resistance already mentioned, one must add resistance *to* transference and also transference *as* resistance. Both possibilities exist, and it is sometimes important to distinguish them.

Many clients want more from the counselor than a professional helping relationship. They want a "real" relationship. They have an emotional need to feel that their responses in the relationship arise from the actualities of the present. In varying degrees they may be unable to accept the notion that they are reacting to the counselor *as if* he were a parent; instead, they insist that he become or be the parent!

Such clients will tend to deny transference phenomena and resist clarification or interpretation of them. On the contrary, they will do everything in their power to make the professional relationship a personal one. They may demand all sorts of proof that they are *really* accepted. They tend to "move in" on the counselor—to the point that he may feel absorbed, consumed, or "devoured"—and will invite the counselor to reciprocate.

The counseling relationship is a real relationship, but it is one that requires some distance if it is to be therapeutic for the client. The "hunger" for more than the professional relationship tends to disrupt the treatment. This "hunger" may exist in the counselor as much as in the client. It is the counselor's task to recognize this, and at the same time to preserve the relationship for the sake of the therapy. Also, the counselor will recognize that some clients are too sick for counseling and will never tolerate the "distance" in the relationship required for effective therapeutic work.

Transference becomes a resistance for quite similar reasons. Once transference reactions to the counselor are established, it may be very difficult for the client to give them up. It feels safer and more gratifying to go on in this relationship than to use it for purposes of insight and growth as applied to current problems. Subtle transferences sometimes produce these difficulties. The client takes the interviews as offering permanent support, or as permission for all sorts of behavior not intended by the counselor. Or, by way of contrast, the friendly and objective counselor goes on for months not realizing that he is *heard* by the client as critical and directive. It is disillusioning but true that the benevolent and accepting counselor, who loves his fellowman and is only trying to do a job, is nevertheless perceived by his client as having horns and a tail!

Such transferences can be pointed out, if they are detected. At other times they never come to light. In counseling, they may make for interminable relationships, mutually frustrating at times; more often, perhaps, they terminate the therapy under more or less mysterious circumstances. Sudden and intense transference reactions account for many early dropouts, often after one interview. Some of these are inevitable; others will be prevented when we learn more about communication—verbal and nonverbal—with all sorts of clients coming for help under all sorts of conditions.

E. *Countertransference*

There are numerous definitions of *countertransference*. These vary from the psychoanalyst's *unconscious* reactions to his patient's transferences in the psychoanalytic situation to *all* of a therapist's reactions to a client or patient in any professional helping relationship. There is great diversity of opinion and advice as to what one should (or can) do about countertransference.

There is nothing one can do about *unconscious* reactions to patients or clients. If one is not aware of them they are not subject to volitional inspection or control. One can *suspect* the presence of countertransference, however, if—as suggested earlier—one is unaccountably uncomfortable with a client; i.e., sleepy, bored, uneasy, vaguely apprehensive, and so on, or, to list other possibilities, overly protective, reassuring, optimistic, and the like. If one tends to withdraw from the client, if something seems forced, if physiological tension symptoms appear, or if there is something different in one's pattern of relating to a particular client, then one must raise the questions: Is there something unique about this client, or is there something unusual being stirred up in me?

The counselor can, of course, have his own transference reactions toward clients. These are strictly his transferences, not countertransferences. That is to say, these are products of the counselor's own fantasy life or confusion of present with past rather than something predominantly stimulated by clients' transferences to him. It may or may not work, since the whole business is largely unconscious, but the counselor—noting some sort of uneasiness in himself or in the relationship—should at least make the effort to ask himself what is going amiss. Am I seeing in this client a brother, a sister, a parent, some of my own wayward impulses, a strict conscience, or what? Or, if it is really transference that he is reacting to: Am I anxious, angry, or sexually aroused by this client's passive, dependent demands, competitive strivings, sexual teasing, outright seductiveness, or whatever?

A hunting companion once turned to a young married woman and said, "Mrs. Jones, why are you so seductive?" The woman was aghast. Consciously she was being her usual social self. Unconsciously, it turned out, she wanted very much to be admired, to attract as much attention from as many persons as possible. This was more pregenital, narcissistic than genital in its motivations. In a sense, neither hetero- or homosexuality was important.

A young woman client who never dated boys spoke haltingly in disjointed and colorless sentences. The counselor was bored and sleepy, and not a little guilty. Case material indicated that the client's manner of speech was in part related to "hidden" concerns about what might happen on dates. She spoke much more freely on neutral topics. It seemed clear that this boring talk was a defensive operation on the client's part, and that the counselor's reaction of boredom was in part an "appropriate" response to such a defense and in part her own defense against suppressed frustration and repressed rage at such a difficult and unresponsive client.

Transference and countertransference are at work when a counselor and client spend much of their time talking about how difficult or wicked is the client's spouse. They have made a tacit agreement to like each other and to see the principal problems as being with the spouse who, of course, stubbornly refuses to conform to the client's specifications. Something similar happens when everything is blamed onto the past, onto the client's "rejecting parents." This type of solution is very gratifying—Norman Reider has called it a retroprojection—and can go on forever. It may solve the difficulites of the very paranoid individual, but it can be a device for failing to come to grips with current problems. The past should illuminate the present—not obscure it!

The counselor will tend to interact with a client as he does in other relationships. After all, he has the same basic needs and impulses. He differs from the client, however, in being more aware of his needs and impulses, having them under greater self-observation and conscious control and, above all, knowing that they must find gratification in other relationships than those with clients. Natural responses must often become controlled responses. If the client evokes a counselor's protectiveness, the counselor must not be overly protective. If the client attacks, the counselor cannot retaliate. Giving, helping, placating, soothing, punishing, and even mothering have their times and places, but for the majority of clients they are no substitute for a professional friendliness, understanding, mutual respect, and eventual independence.

F. *The Power of Relationship*

It is sometimes difficult for the counselor to take himself as seriously as the client takes him. This is a special aspect of transference-countertransference interaction. The counselor must take himself seriously, and yet avoid the temptation to play the role of the Almighty. He must always be aware of the power of the counseling relationship and equally careful to avoid abusing it.

All of us contain within ourselves a helpless, frightened, superstitious child. When we are sick, the doctor assumes godlike powers and nurses become tender, loving mothers. We are apprehensive and outraged if they fail us in these roles. Our fate seems to depend on whether the apple core hits or misses the wastebasket, or whether a bomb, in combat, has our number on it. Severe stress brings out the best and worst in us, the most altruistic and the most primitive, the most "adult" and the most "infantile."

Despite his grown-up, social facade, therefore, the client with troubles has regressed to greater or less extent. The measure of his regression may well be the degree of his transference expectations of the counselor—the extent, in other words, of his perception of the counselor in godlike proportions. It matters little if the client is a banker in his fifties and the counselor a young woman social worker just out of school; the mantle of power and authority will be on *her* shoulders and the client will tend to react accordingly. The greater the inner helplessness of the client, the more weighted with magic powers—for good or ill—the counselor's every word.

All of this is so easy to forget. The client—a woman, this time—may be sitting there with smiling lips and eager eyes, and there is every temptation to relate to her a little playfully, on the basis of social equality and friendliness. But the ironic word may be taken literally or the light touch may misfire. The client, like the patient in a hospital, may panic because of a chance remark—overheard and misunderstood —from the corridor. It is generally better to assume that the anxious client, like the frightened child, hears things as absolutes: good or bad, black or white, life or death.

The power attributed to the counselor arises, then, from the client's need, confusion, and anxiety. It derives from the child's demand that its parents be all-wise and all-powerful. In such images there is security. The counselor, on his part, must accept this responsibility, but never let it "go to his head." He must, in other words, accept the professional competence that is his, but never overstep it.

It is very flattering to be made a god and put high on a pedestal. One is easily tempted to look down from this lofty perch and to pontificate. It is better to remember that even the needy client has an "observing ego," and that this one has a fishy and jaundiced eye. Gods, like parents, are usually regarded ambivalently. One difficulty about the pedestal is that the higher you are the harder you may fall.

Just as we refuse to accept the lofty position of a god, so do we avoid sharing our problems with the client and assuring him that we, too, are just "poor weak mortals after all." He did not come to help us and, despite some transference attempts to the contrary, he is not genuinely interested in our private lives. Unless he is an extremely deprived person (emotionally speaking), he needs our professional help in solving his problems; not our personal friendship. The counselor is usually correct in offering friendliness but not in offering friendship.

The reason for friendliness is, of course, to make possible a working professional relationship. The client may very well need a sense of acceptance, a welcome, as the basis for entrusting himself to the relationship. The reason for stopping short of friendship, however, is so that transferences can be seen for what they are and thereby used for the client's benefit. The relationship must, so to say, be partly a real relationship and partly not. It is a real *professional* relationship, hopefully characterized by mutual confidence, trust, and acceptance, but at the same time it must have the professional "distance" that permits both counselor and client to become aware of just those irrational, paradoxical regressions, resistances, and transferences that are so important to self-understanding and problem-solving. If the relationship becomes a real one all the way, it may be very gratifying for the lonely or helpless or frustrated parts of the client, but it may well destroy the possibility of his growth and ultimate emancipation from the counselor.

The power of the counseling relationship, then, is power for good or ill. The tides of unconscious childhood strivings are stirred in times of stress. They increase with the arousal of magical expectations in the counseling relationship. They may become even more powerful if the relationship continues for some time and if the ever-present struggle between the infantile longings and the grown-up controls of the client becomes, by transferences, a struggle between client and counselor. Much of the counselor's skill, therefore, is in the recognition, acceptance, and therapeutic use of these irrational forces, in avoiding the pitfalls of shutting them off or unduly stimulating them and, in general, keeping them at optimal levels for therapeutic work.

The power of relationship is also a sustaining power. From the first release of anxieties in an initial interview and the counselor's agreement to share the burden of the client's problems, the relationship becomes a crutch for the client's crippled ego. Ventilation, sharing, clarification, interpretation, problem-solving—all of these, supported by acceptance in relationship, lighten the ego's tasks and enhance its strengths. If all goes well, this crutch, like other crutches, can be put away.

G. *Rules of Thumb*

Concerning Resistances:

1. Initial resistance may be due to the newness of the counseling experience and situation. There may be doubts about the counselor's training and experience, and the confidentiality of what is said. Suspiciousness about records, tape recorders, and so on is not necessarily paranoid, but may be. The client's expectation of being blamed and judged is omnipresent.

2. Do not forget resistance due to "secondary gain." Many problems, no matter how they hurt, have their benefits. The naughty child gets attention, the martyred wife gets sympathy, and the disabled veteran gets compensation. Such gains may hamper counseling and preclude solutions.

3. The counselor does well to ask: "Am I provoking resistance?" How? By being critical, sarcastic, judgmental, overly protective, seductive, obtuse, or otherwise inappropriate to the needs of the client.

4. Regressive and transference possibilities must also be considered.

Concerning Regression:

1. Inconsistent, alternating, or otherwise variable attitudes on the part of the counselor tend to facilitate regressive tendencies in the client. A consistent, accepting professional attitude tends to prevent regression.

2. Valid activity on the part of the counselor—i.e., discussion of current reality problems, clearly indicated interpretations and confrontations about the client's interpersonal and adaptive patterns, and, when necessary, restatement of the limitations of agency function or counseling relationship—tends to prevent regression.

3. Activity that ignores or fails to utilize the client's ego strengths promotes regression. This includes: spoonfeeding, talking down, overprotection, excessive sympathy, being too supportive, participating too early in the client's struggle with a routine problem, cutting off tears, anger, and other expression of appropriate affect.

4. Activity that expresses the counselor's anxiety, need to please, need to mollify, need to smooth over, or need in any way to see the world and the client through rose-colored glasses encourages regression.

Concerning Transferences:

1. The silent counselor, like the silent analyst, encourages transference reactions. The *techniques* of psychoanalysis are designed to permit the development of a transference neurosis. They are generally inappropriate to counseling.

2. Valid activity on the part of the counselor keeps transference to a minimum. While the counselor should be a good listener, he should be active in some way during each appointment, if only to ask a question, seek clarification of a point, or make some summarizing comment at the end.

3. Frequent appointments tend to increase transferences; infrequent ones, to diminish them.

4. The use of free association interviews, attention to fantasies, dreams, and feelings, and minimal participation by an anonymous counselor all facilitate transferences, the more so when everything is sympathetic, permissive, and "understanding." The counselor does not have to reveal himself and "show" that he too is a human being. The best correctives for unwanted transferences are a consistent, professional manner, an orientation to the realities of the counseling relationship and to the realities of the client's problems, and prompt recognition and clarification of the inevitable transferences to any helping person seen as a powerful authority who may gratify or punish.

5. Wording of transference clarification or interpretation may make a difference. Kept at the level of the counseling relationship, interpretations—"You may feel this about me"—may intensify the transference. Give distance—"You might have felt this about X when you were a child" or "Yes, people often feel this way"—and you tend to decrease transferences.

6. Generally speaking, one does not interpret or interfere with a mild positive transference or objectively justified friendly feelings toward the counselor. Such feelings "carry" the relationship and sustain the client through

disagreeable times. An erotic transference, however, hides hostility or strong oral (passive-dependent) demands or something comparable. A hostile transference indicates anxiety, frustration, guilt, or some "defensiveness" for which the counselor or counseling situation may or may not be accountable. Disruptive problems, such as serious illness, facilitate idealization and deification of the counselor, especially physicians; clients or patients must see him that way to feel that they can survive.

Concerning Countertransference:

1. There is no law against liking or disliking people. You may show the former in moderation. If you cannot conceal the latter, it is better to transfer the client.

2. Like a good parent, you can still accept the client even though you may dislike his behavior.

3. It is permitted to *wish* to help people. It is not permitted to *demand* that they be helped. The need to help, the need to cure, the need to rescue—"therapeutic ambition" —is your problem and will frequently cause the client to "run" or to stay and frustrate you.

4. Counselors have all sort of feelings about clients. Only the more intense ones are likely to interfere. Real problems arise when counselors act upon their feelings instead of observing and living with them. A male counselor may note that a woman client is sexually attractive, but he ceases to be a counselor if he becomes sexually aroused and expresses it. He must be able to feel—and rarely say aloud—"Another relationship might be very pleasant, but that is not why we are here." Beware of

this, however; the client may terminate the treatment and say, "Now let's have a date!"

5. Suspect countertransference, whatever your conscious feelings, when you come late, get bored, are distracted, become tense, reassure, overprotect, tell jokes, mollify, or work overtime with any one client. Ask yourself, "Is the client making me feel or act this way?" and also, "Is this a result of some disturbance in me?" The former offers the easy out, but the latter must not be ignored.

6. Finally:
   a. It always takes two for a woman to be seductive.
   b. Never underestimate the power of the Unconscious.
   c. The dazzling smile and dancing eyes most commonly indicate an unconscious wish for mothering.
   d. The "castrating female" is frequently, in part, the creation of a passive-dependent male.
   e. The ultramasculine "he-man" may want a mother as much as the next fellow.
   f. Don't jump to conclusions about overt homosexuality on the basis of external traits or actions. These can be misleading.
   g. When you feel moralistic read the Bible, II Samuel: 11 and 12.

1. Robert Waelder, *Basic Theory of Psychoanalysis* (New York: International Universities Press, 1960), p. 253.

2. Herman Nunberg, *Principles of Psychoanalysis: Their Application to the Neuroses* (New York: International Universities Press, 1955), pp. 245–246.

3. Karl Menninger, *Theory of Psychoanalytic Technique* (New York: Basic Books, Inc., 1958), pp. 83–84.

Part II

COUNSELORS
AND COMMONLY
ENCOUNTERED
PROBLEMS

CHAPTER SIX

Principles to Problems

A. *Shift of Emphasis*

Part I of this book has been concerned primarily with *principles* of counseling. Case vignettes have been used to illustrate these principles, but our attention has been centered upon the phenomena of counseling in general rather than upon any particular problems that clients bring to the counselor. In Part II, the focus shifts from principles to problems.

In making this shift, we do not, however, give up one of the all-important principles of counseling; i.e., that we deal with people. It is not a problem that comes to us. It is, rather, a person with a problem. Carl Binger makes this point most tellingly in his book, *The Doctor's Job*. He refuses to discuss with an eager intern that "case of hepatitis in Room 345" until the intern makes it clear that he wants to talk about "Mrs. Smith, who has hepatitis." We must keep the same perspective as we talk about "the Joneses who are having marital problems" or "Miss Brown who is an unmarried mother."

At the same time, however, it is useful to group the problems that people bring to us. It is a beginning, though by no means the end, of the diagnostic process. We know some of the things to look for in unmarried mothers even though we must avoid the trap of thinking that the label "unmarried mother" establishes more than a symptomatic diagnosis for this particular pregnant and unmarried Miss Brown. The "wife of an alcoholic" is a counseling stereotype, but, again, it points the way to some things to think about rather than to any conclusive formulation as to what kind of person or what kind of marriage we shall be dealing with.

At this point we may ask again, "Who are our counselors and what kind of problems do people bring to them?" Authoritative answers to these questions are in the publication of the Joint Commission on Mental Illness and Health entitled *Americans View Their Mental Health*. Taking into account the broad spectrum of problems for which people seek professional counseling, a statistically representative group turned to various resources as follows: [1]

Clergyman	42%
Doctor	29%
Psychiatrist or psychologist in private practice (or not ascertained)	12%
Psychiatrist or psychologist in clinic, hospital, or other agency	6%
Marriage counselor or clinic	3%
Other private practitioners or social agencies for handling psychological (emotional) problems	10%
Social service agencies for handling non-psychological problems (e.g., financial)	3%
Lawyer	6%
Other	11%

This is the overall picture. Not all counselors encounter

the same problems in the same ratios, of course; but similarities are more striking than differences. For example, 92 per cent of persons consulting a marriage counselor present problems with the spouse or the marriage, and 8 per cent problems involving their children. Other difficulties brought to marriage counselors are not statistically significant.

In the case of doctors (not including psychiatrists), however, 35 per cent of the problems involve the spouse or the marriage; 8 per cent a child or relationships with a child; 5 per cent involve other family relationships; 8 per cent involve problems of job or school; 18 per cent involve matters of personal adjustment; and so on. Thus, the selection of a source of help varies somewhat with the nature of the problem as defined by the client himself. The distribution among the groups of counselors most frequently sought out—clergymen, doctors, and psychiatrists—is quite comparable, except for the fact that the psychiatrists have a proportionately larger number of clients having problems about or with children and with problems of personal adjustment (not primarily vocational).

Without looking further at the matter of who consults whom for what problems, here is the overall picture of the frequency of problems brought by people to the whole group of counselors listed above: [2]

Problem area:

Spouse; marriage	42%
Child; relationship with child	12%
Other family relationships—parents, in-laws, etc.	5%
Other relationship problems: unspecified	4%
Job or school problems; vocational choice	6%
Nonjob adjustment problems in the self	18%

Problem area:

Situational problems involving other people (e.g., death or illness of a loved one) causing extreme psychological reaction	6%
Nonpsychological situational problems	8%
Nothing specific; a lot of little things; can't remember	2%
Not ascertained	1%

In a very rough sort of way, then, we can say, "Here is a marital problem" just as in another setting, we say, "Here is an alcoholic." We should not say these things, however, unless we remind ourselves and our listeners in the same breath that no two marital problems are the same and that no two "alcoholics" are alike. Karl Menninger has written forcefully and eloquently of late about the destructive consequences of pinning labels onto people and then mistaking the label for the person.

The chapters that follow contain brief discussions of commonly encountered problems in counseling. The focus will be on the problems. We shall not forget, however, that these problems are brought to us by individuals and families, and that people having the same difficulties (superficially) are so different in native endowment, intelligence, education, and other life experiences that, in fact, no two persons ever present the same problem. The case vignettes, classified as they are by "problems," will nevertheless illustrate the point that classification is approximate at best and that one always, in the last analysis, has to "get down to cases."

The topics to be discussed here are relatively few considering the variety and complexity of interrelated problems brought to us by clients. Nor can these few matters be dealt with comprehensively. For more definitive, but still relatively short, articles about these and other related subjects, the reader is referred to *The Encyclopedia of Mental Health*.[3] This is the only resource of its kind, and it should be available to every counselor. In the "A" listing alone there are chapters on abortion, adoption, the aging, alcoholism, and anxiety. There are references to other authoritative writings in these fields and a comprehensive bibliography.

B. *Stress*

Stress is a common denominator of all problems. As the term is commonly used, the source or cause of stress is regarded as the stress. Properly speaking, stress is the total situation of stimulus or "cause," the person so affected, and his adaptive or other responses to such (disturbing) stimulation. If we were to maintain the analogy from physics, we would speak of stress as whatever tends to disturb a "vital balance," and strain as the resulting disturbance with which the organism has to cope.

In any case, we may consider both *causes of stress* and *stress reactions*. Roughly speaking, as we have seen, causes of stress may be within ourselves or they may come from the external environment. Also, they may be conceptualized in predominantly psychological, interpersonal, sociological, or biological terms. And when we are at our diagnostic best, we evaluate the interaction of all spheres in the functioning of the total personality.

Stress reactions may be classified as adaptive, defensive, or disorganized. Menninger, as we have seen, speaks of coping, i.e., adaptive reactions within normal limits, and of five orders or stages of dyscontrol beyond normal limits. These include a variety of defensive and disintegrative phenomena. It is here, of course, that we find what we more commonly speak of as symptoms and problems. It is in this sense, accordingly, that stress (including stress reactions) is a common denominator of whatever problems clients bring to us.

C. *Anxiety*

Anxiety is an important stress reaction. It is another common denominator of most, if not all, problems. To the extent that stress is experienced emotionally, it is expressed as anxiety. It must be emphasized, however, that the anxiety need not be overt or conscious. Indeed, we usually deal with anxiety so spontaneously and rapidly that reactions to stress, rather than showing as naked anxiety, appear instead in the form of "anxiety equivalents," defenses against anxiety, or ways of discharging anxiety in some sort of activity that alleviates or gets rid of it without our having to experience it consciously.

Anxiety is subjectively experienced as fear, dread, fright, or panic. It is, in effect, the reaction to impending disaster without actual external threat; as if, for example, we stepped on a rattlesnake where there is no rattlesnake. An "anxiety attack," when it does occur, mobilizes all of an individual's resources for flight or fight. He may sweat, palpitate, and look wide-eyed. He may rush off to eat or drink. He may have a tantrum. He may withdraw or destroy. He is likely to use any means available to him to get away from this most dreadful of emotional states.

Habitual or long-standing ways of dealing with anxiety are more familiar to us. These are the problems of the following chapters. These are the inhibitions, the flights, the excessive demands, the "acting out," and other personality quirks and traits that cause concern to clients or to those around them. These are also the phenomena of the initial interview and the ways of relating to the counselor that so often become problems in themselves. Very simply put, then, stress breeds anxiety and anxiety breeds symptomatic behavior, and it is in this sense that anxiety, too, is a common denominator of the problems that counselors are called upon to treat.

Two important types of anxiety may be labeled "situational anxiety" and "neurotic anxiety." They are not mutually exclusive, but the distinction is useful. The former is related to something definite, is near the surface, and is usually available for interpretation. The latter is generally long-standing, strongly defended against, and not readily interpreted.

Situational anxiety is the anxiety of the initial interview, a reaction to a new, strange and, to the client, unpredictable relationship. It is the anxiety of a patient about to have an operation and is compounded of realistic fear and superstitious childlike fantasies of unknown dangers and disastrous consequences. At the extreme, the client is "paralyzed with fear" and is almost literally blind, deaf, and dumb. The counselor must, if necessary, tell the client that he is "scared to death," accept the fact, get him to talk about it, and help him sort out what is rational from what is fantastic.

Neurotic fears are generally vague and more mysterious. The situational stimulus, if any, is a pretext, not the fundamental source of the anxiety. Childhood factors play a greater role, and the crucial conflicts are intrapsychic. Neurotic inhibitions and symptomatic defense mechanisms are the outward expression of such conflicts, while their true nature and the intense anxiety associated with it are more or less successfully repressed. Whether these can be interpreted and worked through in counseling will depend, as we have seen, on the depth of the repression or, better, on the strength of the defenses.

D. *Defenses and Symptoms*

There are normal and abnormal ways of handling anxiety and other stress reactions. These will not be considered in detail here because they are part of the basic training of most counselors. It will serve our present purpose to remind ourselves, in effect, that there are defenses that work and defenses that do not, and that when they fail, symptoms appear. This point of view is essentially the same as Menninger's in *The Vital Balance* and in any other dynamic conception of human personality that sees the "abnormal" as the signs and symptoms of the progressive failure of normal coping mechanisms.

Repression, when it works, is a normal defense mechanism. It enables us to "forget" what has been painful. Without it we would be constantly aware of a host of feelings of loss, deprivation, hatred, jealousy, shame, guilt, and anxiety from early childhood to the present. When repression fails, or threatens to fail, then other mechanisms are accentuated —projection, for example—or new and symptomatic defenses take over.

Sublimation, inhibition, rationalization, and, to some extent, projection are some of the other defenses that are or may be "within normal limits" and that contribute to normal functioning. Sublimation involves the use of socially acceptable expression of otherwise forbidden or personally unacceptable drives. Games as a "moral equivalent" for war are an example. A number of pregenital, infantile interests and behaviors find sublimated expression during later childhood and beyond.

Without some inhibition we could not endure or be tolerable in family life or larger community living. It is only excessive or unnecessary inhibition that becomes a problem. Rationalization helps us to preserve our sanity. Much of what we do is done for unconscious reasons, but rationalization supplies conscious reasons that reassure us that we do know the score. Rationalization, in a word, protects us from the anxiety of the unknown.

Projection saves us from ourselves. It is not we who are dirty, lascivious, covetous, or destructive; rather, it is those people across the street or across the tracks or across the ocean who have these wicked and vicious traits. Projection breeds prejudice and is socially an undesirable defense, but it protects the individual's self-esteem and, as a group phenomenon, makes group living more tolerable. *We* are OK and love each other; we hate only the stranger or the enemy. This way of handling conflict, of resolving ambivalence, of maintaining self-esteem, and of promoting harmony within the immediate group is so ubiquitous that we must consider it a normal defense and, within limits, a successful one.

Conditions of unusual stress intensify stress reactions and generate unaccustomed degrees of anxiety. Such a situation is marked by an accentuation of normal defenses (repression, denial, projection, inhibition, for example), and by the production of new and symptomatic compromise formations. Some states of dyscontrol are a mixture of the symptoms of partial disintegration and of frantic reconstructive efforts. Regressive reactions, for example, are not merely a retreat from present-day harsh realities, but are also an attempt to find stability at an earlier, but once successful adaptive level, utilizing patterns of adaptation appropriate to that level.

The problems that people bring to us as counselors, therefore, can be seen collectively as stress reactions. In particular, they are ways of coping, or unsuccessfully trying to cope, with anxiety or related overpowering affects, shame, guilt, fear, or loss. If the anxiety is discharged or "acted out" in socially destructive or self-destructive behaviors, we have such problems as crime, delinquency, addiction, alcoholism, and so on. If regressive or unresolved childhood expectations and demands express themselves principally within a marriage, then it is marital problems that we see. Vague personality problems, problems of vocational or educational adjustment, and related matters are often the products of neurotic fears or of long-standing inhibitions. In the broad view, we deal with stress and stress reactions. In the office we deal with Mr. Smith or Mrs. Jones. In between are more or less typical "problems" that people bring to us, and it is to some of these that the following chapters are devoted.

1. Gerald Gurin, Joseph Veroff, and Sheila Feld, *Americans View Their Mental Health*. Joint Commission on Mental Illness and Health. Monograph Series, No. 4 (New York: Basic Books, Inc., 1960), p. 307.

2. *Ibid.*, p. 347.

3. Albert Deutsch and Helen Fishman, eds., *The Encyclopedia of Mental Health*. Six Volumes. (New York: Franklin Watts, Inc., 1963.)

CHAPTER SEVEN

Marital Conflict and Divorce

It is impossible to catalog all of the reasons for marital conflict. They run the gamut from simple innocence about sexual matters to the most complex mental disorders. The presenting problems—not always the most basic ones—include difficulties about money, in-laws, child care, respective roles of husband and wife, sexual adjustment, and a host of others. There is a tendency these days to expect the ideal sexual adjustment in marriage, but it is well to remember that the sexual adjustment is a psychosexual one; that is to say, the sexual life is a mirror of the total relationship between marital partners.

Marital conflicts may be broadly classified as: (1) those arising from external (environmental) pressures on the married couple; (2) those arising from intrapsychic problems of one or both parties; and (3) those stemming from interpersonal problems. Such a separation of causative factors is, of course, artificial; one generally finds an interaction of intrapsychic and interpersonal problems as well as "in-law trouble" or other environmental factors. Generally speaking, however, the focus of counseling is on the interpersonal aspect of marital problems. Where intrapsychic (neurotic) elements clearly predominate, referral for psychiatric treatment is generally indicated, and psychoanalysis is generally the treatment of choice.

A. *Lack of Sexual Information*

It is hard to imagine, in these enlightened times, that young people can get married without knowing about sex. The fact remains, however, that there are graduates of Radcliffe who claim that they were "never told anything" until the day of their wedding. A young man who was the eldest of eight children and who lived in a large city never consciously saw a pregnant woman until he was twenty-five. A doctor who had done numerous pelvic examinations had never seen (consciously, that is) a clitoris. Sexual ignorance, therefore, can be due to simple inexperience, or it can be due to anxiety and repression. It is almost inconceivable how readily people deny and "forget" the things that bother them.

The premium placed upon good sexual adjustment causes some clients to avoid discussing this aspect of marriage. They are likely to give the impression that there is nothing wrong in this area and to resist talking about it. After all, their self-esteem is at stake, and the feeling—often—that they must always be passionate or potent to be "normal." A frank discussion with an enlightened counselor may, however, give considerable relief if only to bring hidden doubts and fears into the open and see sexual problems in better perspective.

A diagnostic problem, for the counselor, is to what extent "ignorance" is simply that, or to what extent it is neurotic inhibition. The test, usually, is in the client's ability to talk about his problems and to use the relationship and whatever new knowledge is made available to him. With many clients a simple discussion of sexual matters will lead to a revival of facts already known but repressed, and the very permissiveness of the counseling relationship will effect a more relaxed, fresh approach to the sexual aspects of the marriage. Sex is not everything, but it is sometimes remarkable how many tensions and vexations in the home disappear when a couple finds sexual happiness together. When counseling fails, after a reasonable time, referral for psychoanalysis must be considered.

B. *Impotence and Frigidity*

The most important fact about these problems is that they can happen to anyone. They are quite common in the early months of marriage, due largely to overeagerness and inexperience. They occur at times of anger, fatigue, debility, and illness. Sexual intercourse is sometimes expected to heal everything, and failures frequently occur when too much is expected of it. Habitual impotence or frigidity, however, is usually symptomatic of psychoneurotic conflicts—for the most part unconscious—and psychoanalysis is therefore the treatment of choice.

C. *Assorted Immaturities*

Someone has reported hearing this in a marriage service: "Do you, John, solemnly promise to be father, mother, brother, sister, but—above all—husband to this woman?" It is psychologically very sound. Husband and wife do, at times, have to be these things to each other. Troubles arise, however, when the "above all, husband" or the "above all, wife" is forgotten or cannot be fulfilled.

The old dictum, "Love is blind," accounts for numerous marital conflicts. People see what they want to see in a prospective spouse, and then disillusionment sets in. A large proportion of young couples anticipate this, or are wise enough and have humor enough to surmount the problems created by the fantasy. Counseling can help many couples where fantasies die harder but are still available to conscious awareness and interpretation.

Typical examples of marital conflict arising from unrealistic expectations are the following:

1. One or both young people marry to "get away from home." This may be good unless the marriage is expected to be as ideal as the home life was disagreeable. That it can hardly be!

2. The marriage is expected to heal all of the hurts of the past. This is a close relative of Number 1. The hurts often go deeper, however, and the marriage is supposed to offer a sense of acceptance, reassurance, and narcissistic gratification that should be within the individual himself.

3. Marital conflicts arise out of acute nostalgia for some former boy friend or girl friend. This may happen at times of adversity—say the first three months of pregnancy—and may be transient. The past seems so attractive because the present is so difficult.

4. Then there is the old refrain:
   I want a girl just like the girl
   Who married dear old Dad. . . .
   Actually, this is not such a bad idea! Problems arise when she is expected to be *exactly* like Mom in her virtues, but without any of her faults.

   Statistically, marriages to the girl or boy "next door" are the most successful. This is very close to marrying someone like Dad or Mom. That is to say, the ethnic, social, financial, ideological, and other backgrounds are essentially the same. If the parents have been good parents and if the early family life has offered emotional security and the opportunity for growth and for healthy identifications, then—other things being equal—it is auspicious to marry within the same general neighborhood or group.

The need to have things just as they were at home, however, indicates immaturity or neurotic rigidity. By the same token the drive to dissociate oneself from all vestiges of the past and to marry someone as totally unlike the parents as possible is probably a counterphobic gesture or an expression of adolescent rebellion or even deeper neurotic hostility. The spouse, in such marriages, usually proves to be the "forbidden" or "rejected" parent in disguise, and the marriage becomes an arena for the ambivalence of unresolved ties to the parental images.

5. Young married persons sometimes find it difficult to let go of certain adolescent relationships and interests. Such interests may represent aim-inhibited sexual strivings and betray emotional unreadiness for marriage. Old friends and old interests can be retained, of course, but a new balance of time and energies must be worked out that takes into account the legitimate claims of the spouse. Some people struggle long and hard to be married and unmarried at the same time!

6. There is a kind of "doctor-nurse" or "boss-secretary" marriage that sometimes seems to be marriage

a la mode. It occurs when one seemingly strong, adequate, and helping person marries another strong, adequate, and helping person, and then it turns out that both (unconsciously) expect to be taken care of. The "doctor" who, after all, takes care of others all day wants to be "nursed" when he comes home at night, and the "nurse" who, after all, has been taking care of the children all day, wants to be the "patient" when her doctor comes home. Thus, the superficial strengths are thrust aside, and the marital conflicts spring from a tug of war over gratification of passive, dependent "oral" strivings.

7. Something of what has just been described is in every marriage. Frequently, however, the gratifications cease when the children come. Then the husband—more often than the wife, perhaps—feels left out, and the wife complains that she has one child more than she actually has. Such situations can be very complicated, but at the same time may be greatly helped by clarification of such issues as to whether husband and wife are expecting too much of each other, are too closely attached to the children, are driving themselves unnecessarily in the home or out of it, and so on.

8. "Mixed marriages" offer special problems. These are marriages between partners of markedly different background—whether because of race, color, religion, social status, or whatever combination of these. It would be too much to say that such marriages are always "neurotic," but they frequently are. The problem is not simply that sexual attraction is the principal basis for the mar-

riage. Actually, the unconscious basis of the marriage is more likely to be an unresolved attachment to and rebellion against the parents. To the extent that both partners are attempting to repudiate their backgrounds, they have a somewhat "guilty" marriage; often they have married a "forbidden love object" in several senses of the word. For these and other reasons both partners are hypersensitive about acceptance by the other, each one mirroring the doubts of the other. Acceptance in the community is an added problem, since some segments of any community will be tentative, if not suspicious, about any atypical marriage, and there will doubtless be actual as well as fantasied indications of rejection.

9. Despite the "sexual revolution" of the past few decades, marriages continue to be fraught with sexual problems. A generation of "emancipated" parents who run around in the nude can frighten their children as much as if they threaten dire punishments for genital manipulation. A revolution in behavior does not necessarily bring with it a revolution in spirit and, indeed, may only confuse the issues. For reasons too varied and complex to analyze—except in individual situations—the war between the sexes seems to be more serious than it ever was and the homosexual titer higher. The sexual problems of marriage remain, therefore; but they are less those of ignorance, inexperience, suppression, and inhibition, and more those of characterological confusions, misidentifications, and pregenital frustrations. All of this, too, is partly a matter of age, education, and socioeconomic

status, and so—as usual—every case of marital conflict has to be considered anew and on the basis of the individuals actually involved.

10. The "child-centered home" presents complex problems. It is the result, sometimes, of parents intimidated by books and articles on child rearing. More often, however, the parents are overly ambitious and perfectionistic to begin with and only select those books that support their preconceived intentions. The child must be a credit to his parents, and one can always find a book with appropriate prescription!

The child-centered home is both the cause and the result of marital conflict. The home must be adapted to the reality needs of infants and young children, of course, and it is only immature parents who cannot accept the inevitable adjustments. The husband or wife who pays undue court to son or daughter invites jealousy in the spouse. A narcissistic parent feeds on the responsiveness of the infant or the adoration of the child. The unresolved Oedipal conflicts of the parents, oddly as it may seem, can be expressed toward son or daughter.

Marital conflicts cause unwise parents to turn to their children for solace. They confide too much and bid too much for sympathy. They get at each other through the children, use them, manipulate them, exploit them—and cause no end of damage. This type of child-centered home is especially vicious.

Since the counselor's focus is on interpersonal aspects of a marriage, he must somehow get "both sides" of the story. This is difficult if only one of the contending partners asks for help. This is particularly so if the client's complaint is about some misbehavior on the part of the spouse. It may be taken as a rule of thumb, however, that there is a fifty-fifty responsibility for marital conflicts and it frequently happens that what the client complains about most vehemently gives him or her considerable unconscious gratification.

The late A. A. Brill, a pioneer American psychoanalyst, once told of a couple who consulted him about marital strife. After a few minutes' restrained talk, they broke into a violent argument using—said Dr. Brill—some of the filthiest language he had ever heard. After this he sent them on their way. Who was he, concluded Dr. Brill, to interfere in such a happy marriage!

The point is that some extremely "bad" marriages are mutually gratifying for those particular couples. The "wife of an alcoholic," a social-agency and psychiatric-clinic stereotype, returns time after time about the problems of her husband's drinking. Gradually it becomes clear that (1) she gets vicarious (unconscious) pleasure from his passive, dependent "oral" gratifications; (2) that she enjoys her superior and dominant position vis-à-vis his "weakness"; (3) that she cannot tolerate a mature husband and can allow herself only a "helpless child"; or (4) that she unconsciously delights in seeing her husband destroy himself. Such clients have their own emotional needs in the counseling relationship, and they frequently resist changing the status of the marriage. If such marriages are to change, one or both partners must be analyzed; and the result is frequently the dissolution of what was, to begin with, an extremely neurotic relationship.

These most difficult types of marital conflict are mentioned to warn the counselor against certain preconceptions. He must not expect to "save" all marriages. He must not assume that superficially "bad" marriages can always be improved. He must not be discouraged if people in marital conflict, despite the clarification of their behavior patterns, go on behaving in most senseless and irrational ways. In some cases, the unconscious forces and intrapsychic conflicts of the marital partners will prevail, and the only therapy that offers some hope of success is that which plumbs the unconscious depths.

D. *Divorce*

Divorce is generally the culmination of marital conflict. In exceptional cases divorce occurs without significant conflict between the partners (as with an infertile partner or one who has become a "vegetable" following brain damage). All too often, however, there is disruptive conflict, and it frequently continues after the divorce. Clients with a history of previous marriage are often in conflict about two marriages, one supposedly past and one current.

A high percentage of divorces occurs nowadays among those who have rushed into marriage—or been rushed by pregnancy—before completing high school or immediately after graduation. Those who marry under the age of twenty-two have a higher divorce rate than those who wait a little longer. Except for farmers, the lowest divorce rate is among professional and business (management) groups. There are important religious factors, of course; Jews and Catholics have far fewer divorces than Protestants.

There is no necessary correlation between marital conflict and divorce. Couples in serious marital conflict may not divorce for financial, religious, business, or professional reasons. Someone has said, "Psychoanalysis is less expensive than divorce," and certainly counseling usually is. The emotional, social, and other "costs" can be very high, but so can those of protracted wedded warfare. The choice can be dreadfully difficult.

Couples sometimes stay married "for the sake of the children." This is a dubious reason, and must be carefully explored. In the first place, it may be a rationalization for various wishes to avoid divorce. Sometimes there are compatibilities in a marriage that conflicts obscure, and counseling may be needed to reveal them. If, on the other hand, the marriage is really nil, then children should not carry the burden of destructive interaction. The primary relationship must be the marriage, and the family stands or falls with it. The wise counselor has no preconceptions, then, about "preserving a marriage for the sake of the children."

Divorced persons have a way of perpetuating their problems. As indicated above, a divorce frequently fails to end the marriage. One young man divorced his wife and then married her best friend, only to be plagued with doubts soon after. Another had several marriages, and always "checked in" with his first wife, as if he had to have her approval to marry again. Numerous couples are divorced and remarried, sometimes several times. Second marriages often see a repetition of the first because the unconscious forces that make for problems have not changed. Edmund Bergler wrote a book, *Divorce Won't Help*,[1] to underscore this point. Because it is the children who are so frequently the footballs of these postdivorce struggles, it is an important task of counseling to expose the destructive interaction and to help the contending parents bring their emotional relationships in line with the legal one.

Children are "caught in the middle" of marital conflicts, separations, and divorces in numerous other ways. The normal childhood fantasies of taking one parent away from the other is accentuated by the reality of their dissension. A nine-year-old girl whose parents were at odds to the point of separation announced that she was going to marry her daddy, and hotly defended her position by citing child marriages in India. It is not uncommon for each parent to try to get the children on his side at times of conflict; and what passes for an attempt to reassure the children of their love becomes more of a courting of the children that only plays into the latter's fantasies of driving a wedge between the parents. What the parents should do, ideally, is to talk with the children together—in terms appropriate to their ages—and tell them of the situation.

Most children need the reassurance that the divorce is not because they have been bad or because of their fantasies or because one parent wants to destroy the other. Ideally, in fact, the parents should break the news as a joint decision, and then give the children a chance—through counseling—to air their feelings and fantasies about the whole situation. During marital crises leading to divorce, the children are likely to get an unaccustomed amount of attention from both parents, and since a variety of parental motivations enter into this, and a variety of responses are stirred up in the children, it is good preventive mental health for the children to talk with a neutral, professional person.

E. *Brief Case Records*

As they come to a counselor, marital problems take many forms and, sometimes, disguises. Here is a fragment of one case:

Mrs. M. came to a public agency for financial assistance. After a dull married life of about twenty years, she left her husband and several adolescent children to move to another city with a man who had seemed to her to be everything her husband had not been. This man proved a great disappointment to her, but continued to exercise a fascination over her. She remained with him and bore him two children, now six and eight. For the past year, however, she has refused to live with him and rarely permits him to visit the children. She has joined a religious cult and is quite active in its work. She often discusses the sins of her neighbors and expresses the hope that they will be "forgiven and saved."

Although we do not know the details, we may assume that this woman is following some unconscious will-o'-the-wisp. She has partially solved her problems in joining a religious cult and by projecting guilt for her own wayward behavior onto her "sinful" neighbors. She does not seek help for her marital failures, and has no conscious need for a solution other than the one she has.

Another vignette follows:

Mrs. C. comes to the agency requesting help with a marital problem. At first she cannot put her finger on any particular difficulty, but she is sure the marriage cannot continue if she does not have help. She and Mr. C. have no "mental activities" in common; in fact, they simply are not matched at all. Later it appears that Mr. C. is excessively demanding, resentful of the children, irregular in his work, withholding of his money, and disposed to become ill when any demands are made upon him. In the course of the interview it also emerges that Mrs. C. identifies herself with her children, putting them ahead of the husband so that they may have "all the advantages that she never had." She was used to a large home, privacy, and other luxuries, but married impulsively to get away from a harsh father. She resents her husband's dependent tendencies, but is herself unskilled in housekeeping. The interview enables her to clarify her feelings, and she decides to separate from her husband, seek a divorce, and return to at least temporary dependence on her own parents.

Analysis of the material indicates that Mr. and Mrs. C., although presenting the outward appearance of mature and adequate persons, each entered marriage with strong dependent wishes for which the other seemed to offer an opportunity for gratification. The emergence of these passive-dependent strivings after marriage soon brought about an impasse, marked by a struggle on the part of each to compel gratification from the other. With mounting frustration and hostility, friction increased until Mrs. C. took the initiative in seeking a way out, but it involved "going home" to her parents.

The following situation involves a twenty-two-year-old wife, the client; a nineteen-year-old husband; and their two-year-old baby:

Mrs. F. made personal application for assistance in finding employment. She stated that her husband never had a job for long and that he has been trying to persuade her to give up the baby so that he will not have to be responsible for her. For some time now Mr. and Mrs. F. have been living apart with their respective parents. He has a chance to travel as a salesman, and wants her to give up the baby and join him. Mrs. F. refuses to do this and wishes to find a job. She did not ask for financial help as she has a little money from pawning a typewriter. She had a very severe father who used to whip her, and now she "becomes so weak" at the thought of being hurt that she cannot defend herself when her husband strikes her. He is described by several persons, including Mrs. F., as mentally brilliant but stubborn, irresponsible, highly sexed, and cruel. He amuses himself by tearing flies and worms apart and is sadistic in sexual intercourse. He is physically immature for his age and has had homosexual relations with his father and with younger boys. He continues to be dominated by his father and has never been self-supporting. Mrs. F. is also physically undeveloped, shy, and diffident about meeting new people. She resents being "babied" by her stepmother, but reacts childishly to delays and frustration—pouting, acting "hurt," and giving up easily. In interviews she has ventilated her hostility toward parents and husband and made some plans for her future security. She becomes indecisive and unable to face the prospect of supporting herself, and with each change feels so insecure that she runs back to her husband rather than face life alone.

One gets the impression here of two babes in the woods, clinging to each other in dependent terror. Mr. F. is clearly psychosexually immature, sadistic, and perverse. Mrs. F., despite some outward reaction against dependence, is nevertheless quite helpless and unable to achieve independence. At deeper levels, it seems clear that she has a strong masochistic attachment to her husband, as she must have had also to her brutal father, so that her marriage is not without unconscious sources of gratification. There is also evidence of a need to dominate and punish Mr. F., as a father-surrogate, and this consumes most of what aggressiveness she has. The counselor hopes to help Mrs. F. to obtain a more objective picture of her situation so that she may decide for herself whether to accept Mr. F. as he is, or leave him. Mr. F. refuses angrily to have any contact with the agency.

Examples and cases of marital discord could be multiplied indefinitely. It is well known that the "causes" and conditions of strife between husbands and wives range from the sublime to the ridiculous. Records of divorce proceedings are full of them. The reader is solemnly advised to study not only the learned treatises on the subject, but also Ann Landers and other "advice to the lovelorn" columns in the daily press. Much can be learned from reading between the lines of such accounts and by going behind the facade of the professed woes and complaints to the tacit assumptions and unconscious preconceptions of those who are having marital difficulties. The "commonsense" therapy of newspaper columnists is sometimes not without its virtues, but all too often it is necessary to go beyond verbal spankings or words of cheerful exhortation and get to the deeper strivings and motivations so often in conflict between husband and wife.

F. *Rules of Thumb*

1. People generally deserve the marriages they make. This sounds judgmental, but it is meant to sound a note of caution against too much sympathy for the client. One must look for the unrealistic expectations or the hidden satisfactions that may lie behind complaints. The martyred client often deals out more punishment than he suffers.

2. The responsibility for marital conflict is fifty-fifty until proven otherwise!

3. The complaints of either spouse are frequently projections. They may be documented and therefore

fact, but they may be projections all the same. In other words, both partners may have the same problems, each seeing them only in the other one.

4. There is neurotic interaction in most marriages, but also a neurotic balance. A change in one partner implies change in the other, and may require it for a new balance. Unless both partners are helped with marital problems, one may sabotage the treatment of the other.

5. Divorces are seldom emotionally final. Friends and neighbors can avoid involvement, but children need protection. Direct counseling is often indicated for them.

G. *Summary*

Despite the complexity of marital problems, counseling has much to offer. It has been estimated that up to 75 per cent of persons in serious marital conflict can be helped significantly if they will discuss their problems with a professionally trained counselor. As with other personal problems, the clarification and greater objectivity that comes from "just talking" to a relatively neutral and uninvolved third person sometimes works miracles.

If the counseling experience reestablishes communication between a feuding husband and wife, this alone may turn the tide. Clarification of unrealistic expectations is frequently valuable. The extent to which a spouse is expected to be just like a parent, or the precise opposite of a parent, or both at the same time, can be brought into conscious awareness quite easily at times; but at other times, never. The same is true for unconscious expectations that the marriage will heal all of the hurts and frustrations of the past.

The problem for the counselor is not so much that many behavior patterns are repressed or unconscious, but rather how deeply repressed they are or how strongly defended against. If the client is clearly psychotic or psychoneurotic, he should be referred at once to a psychiatric resource. With other clients, however, the question is open to discussion; can they make use of counseling or not? Here a trial period is justified and only time will tell.

From what has just been said, it should be clear that the counselor—like any other therapist—must perforce be tentative in his diagnosis and suspend judgment as to therapeutic expectations. He will be able to help some, but not others. Some "bad" marriages will continue because the unconscious gratifications will defy his efforts at clarification and are too powerful to be influenced. Some divorces will occur despite the best efforts of any therapist to preserve the marriage. It seems obvious that some divorces *should* occur, but some will and some will not, whatever the feelings of the counselor. As always, our task is to help people to an awareness of their motives, their feelings, and their goals; and what they do with whatever they discover about themselves is something that (with rare exceptions) we have to accept, whatever our own preconceptions.

1. Edmund Bergler, *Divorce Won't Help* (New York: Harper & Brothers, 1948).

CHAPTER EIGHT

Children and Parents

A. *Problems With or About Children*

Children comprise nearly one-half of the world's population, and their frequently harassed parents account for perhaps one-fourth. Their mutual problems are not so numerous, happily; but 12 per cent of requests for help center in a child or in parental relationships with children. The range, scope, and variety of problems in this area are inevitably beyond detailed consideration here. The emphasis in this chapter is, rather, on what most frequently become the counselor's problems.

Some years ago a book entitled *The Rights of Infants*[1] was followed by an article called *The Rights of Parents*. The former is an extremely important work, but its title became a symbol for the so-called child-centered home. Parents became so fearful of doing the wrong thing, it was alleged, that little joyousness remained in marriage or in parenthood. The cure for children's problems threatened to become worse than the disease!

Another statement of this misguided point of view was: There are no problem children, but only problem parents. One young mother handled this guilt-ridden situation by asserting, after having read all of the baby books, that she intended to do everything right, including making all of the right mistakes. Considering how the child turned out, her system was effective.

The truth is that there are both problem parents and problem children. "As the mother goes, so goes the child," is largely true for infants, and becomes progressively less so as the child develops. Even the child of two has a vivid psychic life of his own, and his understanding of events, embroidered as it is by fantasy and magical thinking, is a vast reservoir of emotional disturbance. In any given situation it becomes a nice diagnostic problem as to how much is contributed by the child and how much by parents or other environmental forces.

Mary E. Bergen [2] has described the psychoanalytic treatment of a little girl who, at the age of four, saw her father stab her mother to death. Her mother's last words, as the child recalled them, were "Get out of here." The child saw neither parent after this bloody scene, the father being committed shortly thereafter as a paranoid schizophrenic. To epitomize a complicated situation, it turned out that the mother's shouted, "Get out of here," was much more traumatic for the child than the murder. The child was accustomed to violence, but the implications, for her, of the mother's angry words, followed by her disappearance, proved to be disruptive to her defensive capabilities.

Sidney Berkowitz once told of a child treated for a school phobia following an accident to her grandmother. The latter, baby-sitting for a few hours, called the child from play. The little girl, angry, wished that her grandmother would fall and break her neck. It happened soon afterward that the grandmother did fall and sustain a fracture, and it was after this that the child, because of her fears, refused to leave the house, lest something happen also to her mother. The counselor had to work, of course, with the child's belief in the omnipotence of her wish, and what turned out to be the principal resistance in the treatment was the child's realization that if she gave up the conviction that "bad wishes" come true, she would also have to give up her belief that "good wishes" come true—at Christmastime, for example. Here again, what the child brings to the "traumatic" situation can be of determining significance.

This is not to deny that there are sick parents, psychopathic parents, and rejecting parents. We have all too much evidence of parents' problems with each other and with their children. What we often forget, however, is to consider how the child views these "problem parents." We certainly cannot assume that the child sees them as we do. His needs and values are not ours, and we must avoid jumping to conclusions as to whether or how "rejecting parents" may be upsetting to a child.

A boy of about ten encountered a little girl at school with a chunk of chocolate. She showed it with a "look what I've got" air and the boy, very envious, said, "What is it, chewing tobacco?" Her crushing reply was, "My father doesn't chew, thank you!" The boy never did know how her father got into that exchange, but we can understand, of course, that fathers—when we are that age—are heroes to us, whatever they may be to the outside world. In any case, we must be as cautious about surmising how a child views even "problem parents" as we are about judging how an adult will react to the divorce of a friend.

Failure to individualize clients takes the form of pinning labels on them. Thus, a "child" can be anyone under twenty-one, depending upon who is talking. There are dangers even in our subdivisions: pre-Oedipal, Oedipal, latency, pubertal, adolescent, and so on. There are valid generalizations, to be sure, about "latency children," but one must remember, as Edith Buxbaum has pointed out, that "latency" is a relative matter. The same is true of "adolescent." The thirteen-year-old girl who angrily but anxiously demands to know if she can go on a double date with some older kids should almost certainly be told, "No"—if for no other reason than her manifest anxiety. A couple of years later, however, a discussion might well be in order, and possibly a different answer. In either situation, much depends upon the emotional development of the girl as well as other relevant factors. We are likely to be suspicious of parents who have all of their children—aged six to twelve—going to bed at the same time, and we have to be careful not to fall into a comparable trap ourselves.

There are also dangers of the opposite sort. Some diagnostic tags are so reprehensible to us that we sometimes avoid facing up to their appropriateness. We would do well to regard any diagnostic term as a temporary working hypothesis. We should keep it to ourselves perhaps and, in any case, be aware of its possible connotations for others. But to fail to have an operational diagnosis can be as fatal as to tag someone with a "hopeless" one.

A fifteen-year-old girl was seen because of suicidal threats and gestures. She was not regarded as psychotic, but several consultants had considered her "immature," "hysterical," and "infantalized by her mother." Questions as to whether she was "retarded" had, for the most part, been avoided or expressed in euphemisms.

Partly because of this she had never had a full battery of psychological tests by a trained clinical psychologist.

This girl had been born two and a half months prematurely. Details of birth were not available, but an eye condition suggested that she had been given too much oxygen either at birth or during the two months that she was in an incubator. She did not walk until two and a half and she did not talk well until five or so. The family situation had been chaotic throughout her life and she had been in difficulties at school (mostly academic) since the early grades. The evidence for early organic brain damage had been minimized in all appraisals of this situation.

To put it in a nutshell, the counselor (and several consultants) failed to raise the fundamental question as to whether this girl was neurotic because organically retarded, or retarded because neurotic, or both! A *practical* diagnosis would have been mental retardation, and it would have been wise to make it, provided the counselor could avoid being hopeless about it, jumping to conclusions as to *how much* retarded, or having preconceived notions as to the relative importance of organic as contrasted to other factors in the total picture.

Such diagnoses must nevertheless be subject to revision:

A case in point was that of a young Marine about to be "surveyed out" of the service with the diagnosis "Dementia Praecox; Schizophrenia." This is one of those hopeless diagnoses that Dr. Karl Menninger rightly insists we should avoid—at least in talking with clients or their relatives. The Marine, nevertheless, had apparently been "schizophrenic" for several days. He had completed a very arduous course of combat training, gone on a picnic, had two beers too many, fallen off the back end of a truck, and bumped his head. A combination of fatigue, beer, and concussion fractured his habitual defenses, and he had what should have been called a "transient schizophrenic reaction." The diagnosis he was given meant a mandatory medical discharge. He did not want this, however, and so his medical officer wrote a "survey" calling for return to duty. Someone in Washington was at least partially convinced, because the Marine got orders for "trial duty" for one year—an almost unprecedented action by the Navy.

B. *School Problems*

The problems of some children and young persons are called "school problems" simply because it is in school that they manifest themselves. Actually, they may be "home problems" that show up away from home, or they may be problems of being in *any* situation except the home. Because school is virtually inescapable, it is the most usual testing ground for adaptations away from home.

School problems (so-called), school failures, and school dropouts—at whatever age and academic level—must be evaluated with respect to the intrapsychic life of the individual concerned, his interaction within his family, and the total setting of the school, be it nursery or graduate school. The patent "separation anxiety" of the young child has its echo in the nostalgia of the beginning college student. Both can be called "homesickness" and may be benign and transient or serious and persistent. The conflict between God and evolution that shattered the emotional tranquillity of generations past has a modern counterpart in the "identity crises" of today's undergraduates who are another "lost generation" in that they hardly know who they are, or why, and have nothing to show for it except a most unpleasant sense of emptiness and spiritual isolation. More of this a little later!

Adverse reactions to starting school at age five or six are common, but usually not serious. Much can be understood in terms of "if the mother is ready to let the child go, the child will be ready to go." This is much too simple a formulation, however, when the problems are mainly in the fantasy life of the child. The so-called "school phobia," for example, often conceals a child's fear that something dreadful will happen *at home* while he is at school, and this in turn may hide unconscious "death wishes" toward parents or siblings.

Learning difficulties stem from many sources. A number of children were unable to learn to read in a school system where teachers, accustomed to "phonetics," were compelled to use other techniques. There is no doubt that some children were thrown into conflict by the teachers' anger, no matter how well suppressed, and by the latent atmosphere of dissension in the schools. Children are as much unsettled by conflicts among the grown-ups at school as among grown-ups at home.

The school "dropout problem" also stems from the home, the student, and the school, in varying proportions with each individual case. Studies at the elementary school level indicate a correlation between parental attitudes toward schools and schooling, and pupils' consistency of attendance. A recent study of college failures indicates that even here the family may be an important factor. Dropping out of college may not be a rebellion against family expectations (as it often is, to be sure), but (unconsciously) an effort to preserve an established balance and harmony within the family.

Studies of high school dropouts indicate that there are two important psychological factors to consider: adolescent rebellion and "success neurosis." These may be opposite sides of the same coin. Rebellion may defy the overt wishes of the parents, but failure (i.e., inability) to go further and do better than others in the family ("success neurosis") may be a compliance with their hidden wishes. The "success neurosis" is largely an intrapsychic matter, to be sure, but the fact remains that the most successful member of any family has to deal with highly ambivalent attitudes on the part of others, and it often feels safer and more comfortable not to be estranged by too much success. Just as the older brother or sister in a family is loved and hated with equal intensity by the younger ones, so will the one who becomes most successful become the target for a mixture of admiration, resentment, and demands that frequently result in alienation. Some would rather fail than destroy a harmony based upon relative equality of fortunes.

A person with "success neurosis" has inner guilts and anxieties to deal with. His unconscious feeling is that he has purchased his success with the destruction of others, including the earliest objects of love, hate, rivalry, and envy, namely his parents or brothers and sisters. If such conflicts are very severe, a person cannot allow himself to be successful. If they are less severe, he can be successful but only at some cost to himself in guilt or neurotic suffering.

Such facts help to explain why the wealthy, for example, tend to live together and associate mostly with one another. It is not simply that they are snobs, which they may or may not be, or that they have much in common apart from their wealth, but—more important, perhaps—that they have less greed, envy, and other forms of hostility to deal with when they are with their "own kind." All of this applies to academic success as well—and to other status differences—inasmuch as knowledge, power, and wealth are all more or less equated, and related to unconscious residues of getting the most in the way of food, love, and approval from parents and other early authorities.

These considerations accentuate, again, the importance of differential diagnosis. School problems are not, simply, the symptoms of inadequate adaptation to hard, competitive, and otherwise stressful educational tasks and other aspects of the academic milieu. The conflict may be basically intrapsychic, but externalized to include the school. Or, intrapsychic, but externalized to include the home and school. Or, it may be principally in the home, in that going to school involves the student in greater conflict within the family than before. So one must ask, together with more usual questions: "What does going to school or college mean to this student and to his family, and what does it do to the preexisting equilibrium within the family?"

C. *Adolescents*

The chief point to be made here about this vast topic is that we must avoid thinking of "the adolescent" just as we must avoid thinking of "the child." Adolescence runs from junior high school to marriage, and sometimes far beyond. It is a succession of developmental experiences and levels, and it is as far as many of us go. In his book *On Adolescence*,[3] Dr. Peter Blos describes the phases of adolescence under the following headings: Latency Period, Preadolescence, Early Adolescence, Adolescence Proper, Late Adolescence, and Postadolescence. Counseling with adolescents requires specialized knowledge and unusual skills, and it is not for everyone! Another very helpful book is Gerald H. J. Pearson's *Adolescence and the Conflict of Genera-*

tions.[4] The author makes the point that even by the time we reach our twenties we repress most of the emotional turmoil of our teens, and that it is therefore extremely difficult to bridge the gap between the generations.

Some aspects of this situation are illustrated by the following:

> These pages were written at an enchanting seaside resort halfway up Vancouver Island, British Columbia. The "background music" one afternoon was a battle royal between two adolescents, boy and girl, and their tense-appearing mother. It was not determined whether the family was American or Canadian, but it doesn't matter.
>
> Daddy was off golfing. Whether it was his idea or theirs, the youngsters had gone out to gather oysters. Daddy had apparently agreed to buy two dozen at ten cents each, but his offspring, in their exuberance, had brought twenty times that number back to their cottage. Now the problem was to shuck them.
>
> The boy and girl got nicely started, but Mom decided that they should work *behind* the cottage. She fussed about the mess, and ordered them to move. This evoked back talk. Mom began shouting, and daughter broke into stormy tears: "Why do we have to move? Why are you so critical? Why can't we do it our way? Why don't you leave us alone?" Such "reasons" as Mom came up with were uniformly countered by "Big deal!" And so it went on for an hour or more.

One can only speculate about the reasons for this mother's intervention. She may have been jealous of what the boy and girl were doing for Dad. She may have been afraid of what "the neighbors would think" about a mess in front of the cottage. She may have been angry that Dad was off playing golf and leaving her alone with the children. There are many possibilities.

But the lamentations of the daughter are universal. They typify the vicissitudes of all adolescents. The reactions may be less violent or considerably more so, but in some measure they are inescapable. The adolescent is neither man nor child, and yet he is in a period of coming to terms both with himself and with the world in which he lives.

The physical and psychological changes of early adolescence are accompanied by a resurgence of both sexual and aggressive drives. These are so strong as to be frightening, and they are usually handled by such devices as self-imposed discipline, seeking group support for both expression and control, accentuation of intellectual defenses, and flight into asceticism. The shame, embarrassment, and general self-consciousness about development of breasts, pubic hair, and other secondary sex characteristics are simultaneous expressions of feeling about the instinctual strivings that underlie these changes.

Increased aggressivity paves the way for academic or vocational achievement, mating, emancipation from the parents, and eventual autonomy. This is the period of stressful interaction with the parents. Neither man nor child, the adolescent is sometimes adult one day and child the next. He needs controls and needs to rebel against them. His personality is still unstructured, unpredictable, and often chaotic. He can riot one week and do good works the next. A model boy sometimes bursts into acts of rape or murder.

The counselor should not treat an adolescent as a child or as an adult. The wise course may be to confess that you don't know how to talk with him, since one cannot win by bluffing. It is generally valid to assume that the facade is some kind of play-acting, an expression of how the adolescent would like to be but without much substance back of it. Generally speaking, the best attitude to take, whatever the content, is that of benevolent but firm authority: frank, consistent, honest, matter of fact, and definite.

The younger adolescent generally needs firm discipline, the older one firm leadership. This is another way of saying that the younger adolescent needs external reenforcement for his controls, whereas the older adolescent must put them to the test and strengthen them by use. Here, particularly, one must individualize the client.

D. *Identity Crises*

One of the problems that plagues our era is uncertainty as to individual identity. Questions as to: Who am I? Where do I belong? What am I supposed to do? How can I find fulfillment? Such questions come frequently to counselors. People go to high school or to college hoping to find the answers, and then develop panic when they do not. Or they marry or take up a profession or have a psychoanalysis, and still feel lost and empty. They have been described as being torn between wishes to belong which, however, seem to promise extinction of individuality, and opposing wishes to be separate and unique which, however, seem only to promise aloneness and depression.

These identification problems are, in part, the product of our times. When people grew up in predominantly rural or small-town communities, close to parents and other relatives and close to their daily work, accepting or rebelling against established authorities of parents, school, and church, then—so the argument goes—their identifications were easier and more distinct and the sense of their own identities more clear-cut. Now, in urban and suburban places, the stimuli are too many and too confusing; there are too many persons with whom to identify, and the most important ones are frequently too blurred in their outlines because they are too remote. Mother may be mixed up about her own identity, and who knows where Father is or what he does. The schools offer little if their authority is weak and if they are uncertain about their role, and the Church—itself fighting for a new identity—may offer even less. Little about the external world promises peace or tranquillity. The individual is left to his own devices to discover, if possible, who he is and what he can do about it. Often enough, he provides himself with a livelihood and a mate, and lives on, feeling largely empty, lost, and alone. The crisis comes when anxiety or depression become too much or when some hoped for solution turns out to be another empty promise.

College students often seek solutions through restless moving. Recent years have seen a tremendous increase in numbers of migrant students. Some attend two, three, or even more colleges and universities, and then drop out or join the armed forces. The majority, fortunately, finally settle down and graduate. Thousands of young men and women—of college age or just beyond—are flinging themselves into voter registration drives throughout the nation or joining the Peace Corps, feeling that here, at last, is something vital for them to do. Less fortunate ones, unhappily, are falling back on riots and destruction.

The late President John F. Kennedy sensed these problems in 1960. His early speeches, however, were a summons to action without a plan. Young people throughout the country listened to his call with mounting tension until finally, late in the campaign, he announced the Peace Corps. The sense of relief was almost palpable; here, at long last, was something specific for them to do. The Peace Corps was imaginative, it was important, it commanded loyalty, it valued their skills, it made them feel wanted, and it crystallized their identities as Americans.

Some of this, of course, is as old as Sin. Adam and Eve

must have had something very like an "identity crisis" when they were thrust out of Eden for daring to oppose the will of God. Refugees and other displaced persons are likely to become depressed or experience other upsetting emotional reactions that are due, in part, to a sense of alienation from the motherland; and they may also undergo feelings of concomitant confusion, if not loss of identity. The difference between this sort of phenomenon and the more current "identity crises" is, however, that between persons who have once had a firm and clear-cut sense of personal identity, but had it threatened by some drastic environmental change, and those, on the other hand, who have grown up with tenuous ego boundaries and a shaky sense of personal identity throughout.

"Identity crisis" is not a clearly delineated diagnostic term. It is applied loosely to anyone who is at odds with himself or the world about his proper role or true vocation in life, to the point of developing marked restlessness, confusion, anxiety, or depression. A certain proportion of "school failures" can therefore be so classified, as well as conflicts in women as to "marriage versus career" or "children versus career." The psychological forces vary. The individual may be engaged in an unconscious struggle against some early identifications. Or, his identity may be weak because early identifications were hazy and conflicting. Or, finally, external pressures may have been such as to threaten even a firmly established identity.

E. *Adopted Children, Foster Children, and Stepchildren*

It may be a mistake to suggest that these children are any different from other children. One important difference, however, is that their problems—if any—are likely to be attributed to their special status whether they belong there or not. Various possibilities must be considered, of course; and *one* of them is that being with parents other then their own has little or nothing to do with any problems that do occur.

Some years ago, *The New Yorker* carried the story of a girl brought up by a stepmother. It was not the usual one of mutual antagonism. Actually, they were very close. The outcome must have been tragic for the girl, however, because her closing, devastating words were something like these: "She devoted herself so much to being a friend that she failed to be a mother." Clearly one does not have to be a stepmother, a foster mother, or an adoptive mother (or father) to make this mistake.

It is true, however, that substitute parents frequently feel "on trial." They are at times unwise in their attempts to prove themselves. Some are afraid of failure and become too strict. Others, fearful of being hated, are not strict enough. The clarification of such feelings of self-doubt and insecurity through counseling will often permit a more relaxed and normal way of dealing with the inevitable problems of any children in any home.

The child makes his own contribution, of course. He has his own fantasies about what has happened to him, and why. He has more reason to idealize what he has lost, perhaps, than a child in his original home. The "normal" child, resentful because of some frustration, may dream of the prince and princess (or Hollywood couple) whose *real* child he is, and who someday will claim him for their own. The child who has known a change of parents or homes has more food for fantasy, more experiences to account for, and, frequently, more disturbing feelings with which to come to terms. All of these, then, may be elements in a given problem situation, so that the child needs counseling as much as the parents.

One boy who had been adopted in his infancy had a somewhat stormy period at age fourteen or so. He had always known that he was a "chosen" child, but he had not been told the whole story of his original parentage. One thing that emerged during this stressful period was a fantasy that he had "wild blood" in his veins and was therefore doomed to be wild. At this point he was given full information, including the fact that the real parents were quite young, unmarried, and unprepared to provide a home for him, but that their "blood" was probably as healthy as any. Actually, the adoptive parents of this boy were overly permissive in general and might well have had similar problems with a child of their own. It is possible that the only difference would have been in the fantasy life of the boy.

Counselors who have not had experience in specialized adoption agencies or other agencies offering protective services for children are—along with many lay persons—sometimes annoyed with all of the "nonsense" involved in foster home placements or adoptions. The procedures seem too precious and the requirements too severe. Granting that this may at times be true, the fact remains that—in an adoption—at least four persons or groups must be protected, not only for the moment but also for the indefinite future: (1) the mother or parents who relinquish a child; (2) the child himself; (3) the adoptive parents; and (4) the community.

The mother who gives up a child must, if possible, know her own mind, work through mixed feelings about her decision, and relinquish all legal and emotional claims upon her child. For the sake of herself, the child, and everyone else, she cannot be permitted to change her mind a year, or ten years, later. For the sake of the child and the adoptive parents, there should be a reasonable "fit" as to general background and level of intelligence. Beyond this, the child should be old enough—a few days, at least—so that it can be predicted with fair certainty that he is free from congenital defects and will be a healthy child of at least average intelligence. The adoptive parents must be given a fair chance of having a normal child and, at the same time, the child must be protected from adoptive parents who insist upon a blue-eyed, China doll or an infant who will save their disintegrating marriage or a child who will be expected to live up to their idealized image of one whom they have lost.

These are just a few of the considerations involved in adoptions. Similar ones arise in connection with removing a child from a "bad home" and making a foster home placement. Stepchildren and "children of divorce" and remarriage may, as has already been suggested, present comparable problems. There are extensive writings upon these matters, and it is the better part of wisdom for a counselor —no matter what his professional training—to recognize his limitations in these areas.

F. *Unmarried Mothers*

Most unmarried mothers are in their teens and may therefore be considered here. Again, many persons are involved:

A professional man learned that his nineteen-year-old daughter was pregnant though unmarried. An early reaction was, "You are trying to disgrace your family." This was doubtless partly true. Another reaction was, "You will have to decide what to do about this pregnancy; we will help you, but the decision must be yours." This was very enlightened, on the surface; but it was really full of anger. He might just as well have said, "You've made your bed, now lie in it." Intellectually he knew all about her emotional turmoil, but he "forgot" about her need for counseling at such a time. Finally, he had the fantasy that she would decide to keep the child and that *he* would have to maintain two homes. When the implications of this fantasy were pointed out to him, he decided that outside professional help was clearly indicated!

Meanwhile, the girl's stepmother, who was equally upset and angry, saw the parents of the putative father of the child. Her idea, apparently, was to force a marriage and then go on from there. The boy was clearly immature and unready for marriage, and his parents had little to offer. The total situation cried out for expert help.

The reasons for unmarried parenthood are as many and various as with any other complex form of human behavior. Premarital and extramarital sexual intercourse is more common than ever before, apparently, and it is not surprising that unwanted pregnancies occur. At times they are simply the unwelcome by-product of pleasure-seeking or of a girl "who can't say No." Girls who are lacking in self-esteem, for real or fantasied reasons, are especially vulnerable; they must "allow sex," they feel, to be popular. Thus, competition for social status and desirable companions may be both a compelling reason and a convenient rationalization.

There are also instances of "facilitation" by one or both of the parents. The "mother of an unmarried mother" is almost a social agency stereotype. She is someone who, for example, waits up half the night in order to quiz her adolescent daughter on every detail of her dates, to the point that the daughter goes out and gets pregnant in anger or, as it sometimes seems, to have more exciting details to feed the mother who is living vicariously through her. In other situations, an "acting out" daughter is attempting to escape from a dominating father or from an overly strong unconscious attachment to her father. The emotional currents in these cases are strong, various, turbulent—and mostly unconscious. Sometimes they can be clarified in counseling relationships; sometimes psychoanalysis is the treatment of choice.

G. *Other Facilitation*

It is not always clear to what extent children do their parents' bidding. It is easy to assert, as some authors do, that every child is in a "double bind"; that is, he is pushed in one direction by what the parent *tells* him to do but in the opposite direction by what the parent unconsciously *wants* him to do. Thus, it is often assumed that whatever a child does is in unconscious obedience to parents' equally unconscious commands.

Difficult as this is, it is still too easy. In the first place, the child has two parents, usually, and on this premise must therefore be thought of as responding to two sets of signals from each. In the second place, there is frequently another "double bind" in the "do as I say, not as I do" type of instruction imparted to children. Still another difficulty is the tacit assumption that a child is a blank tablet for the conscious and unconscious messages of his elders whereas, in fact, he very early develops a mind, a will, and a fantasy life of his own, and is just as likely—at certain ages, anyway—to oppose whatever his parents communicate, unless it happens to correspond with his own predominant needs and wishes.

A case in point was very neatly spotted and resolved by a counselor in a family agency. The mother of two small girls—about seven and nine—came because of constant warfare between the children. Oddly enough, the younger was the more aggressive. She not only fought with her sister but also outperformed her in most of their competitive games. After half a dozen interviews or so, this mother talked about her own early family life and her bitter resentment of an older sister who "always bullied her." It was soon possible to point out to her how much she was identified with her younger daughter, how, in effect, she was reversing the relationship with her own sister, and in what subtle ways she was promoting the very competitive relationship that was the basis of her presenting problem.

It seems self-evident that the mother's facilitation nourished an already vigorous contest. Anyone who has been a younger sibling will recognize the possibility. Another child, however, might have retreated from the situation, unable to stand the gaff, or developed some sort of sickness as an "out."

This is only one small example of the great problem of parents wanting to relive their lives through their children. Such efforts are not always bad, of course. Parental ambitions for children are constructive when they provide opportunities for growth and for a wider range of choices than the parents themselves enjoyed. Such ambition becomes destructive, however, when it becomes a demand rather than a chance, and when the details of the parental blueprint are too finely drawn. Under such circumstances the child has little choice but slavery or rebellion.

We take it for granted that this is a period of great confusion for parents and children. Who is secure in his knowledge of what is "success" and what is "failure," what is "masculine" and what is "feminine," and, in countless ways, what is "good" and what is "bad"? Parents inevitably impart something of their own conflicting notions about these matters and, in addition, often unconsciously demand that the children somehow compensate them for what they (the parents) have experienced as deprivation, frustration, or loss. The son of a Jewish tailor must become a doctor while the son of an Iowa banker must become another banker—or, sometimes, a musician!

A common mistake in counseling is to treat this kind of data from clients as equally relevant no matter who the client is. One should differentiate according to probable degrees of distortion. It is one thing for a parent to become aware, in counseling, that he is exerting certain pressures on a child. It is quite another for a child (or an adult talking about his childhood) to claim that his parents subjected him to certain pressures. In the case of parents talking about current attitudes and feelings of their own there is at least the possibility of relatively undistorted reporting, although the counselor will still have to ask himself how the parents' behavior is interpreted by the child. When it is the child (or former child) talking about his parents, however, one must take into account not only how parental images were experienced at that early time but also retrospective distortions from the present—how the client currently *needs* to view his parents. In a word, a client of any age can no more be objective about his parents than a bride about her "in-laws."

This is not to discourage history-taking! We need to know what we can about family background. It is to suggest, however, that we keep in mind the possibility of special pleading. The client has a need to justify himself, and he may therefore paint the parents as worse or better than they deserve. At the same time, it is one of the commonest pitfalls of those who work with children or deal with data about childhood to become overly identified with the child and to take his side against the parents.

H. *The Sick, Crippled, or Defective Child*

Children's reactions to illness are fairly well understood. Sickness makes a child even more aware than usual of his helplessness, his dependence on his parents. Also, it can make him frightened. Because of such feelings, the sick child is frequently a good child. When he gets naughty again, everyone knows that he is feeling better. This is not a universal rule, of course; the very frightened child becomes disagreeable indeed, and this may or may not be a measure of his illness.

An operation is often taken as a punishment, and hospitalization as an abandonment. The worst fears of childhood are intensified at times of sickness and become more complicated if the household is disrupted. Children require special concern when illness, surgery, or hospitalization coincides with weaning, toilet training, or the birth of siblings. Such events combine, for the child, deprivation coupled with punishment for all of the resentful feelings associated with the deprivation. Older children experience these things less in terms of what is done to them by others, and more—internally—as punishment by God or conscience for whatever has been cause for guilt.

Counselors are generally less familiar with the fantasies and feelings of parents who have a crippled or defective child. The acutely sick child evokes worry, anxiety, and even death wishes, but these soon pass away as others share the responsibility for the sickness, and the crisis of the sickness itself passes into convalescence. With chronic illness or permanent defect, however, the parents brood upon what Fate has done to them, and they are likely to be angry, guilty, or depressed.

It is impossible for a parent to avoid the feeling that a crippled or defective child is some kind of reflection on him, somehow his fault, or some punishment for his sins. He will blame it on his adolescent masturbation or other sexual "sins" of youth. He will examine the family tree and attempt to blame heredity. He will become suspicious of his wife or hold her family somehow responsible. He will cry out to God, asking what he has done to deserve such punishment; and at the same time find a dozen reasons within himself as to why he does. As various defenses come into play, he will minimize the problem or deny its existence altogether. He will make all of the mistakes that counselors are trained to avoid; pay too little attention, pay too much attention, overprotect, "business as usual," and all the rest. He will, in short, regard this blight upon the family as he would a cancer within himself. Acceptance of reality and rational behavior require almost superhuman powers.

One family keeps a defective child at home. They sacrifice their freedom and require their other children to do the same. Their position is that this is their fate, and that their children must learn to accept life as it comes. Another family places a defective child in a public institution. They "forget" the child for months on end, and then reproach themselves for doing so. They feel ashamed at having a "public charge" and of shirking their personal responsibility. They wonder if they and their children should not sacrifice whatever it takes for the defective one to have the family life they could provide. These are extremely difficult emotional and moral problems. Who can say *a priori* which are the stronger parents or which are doing the greatest good for the greatest number? The counselor can only be aware of their agony, and help them to arrive at whatever decision is compatible with their lives and their moral sentiments.

I. *Rules of Thumb*

1. The younger the child, the more his problems mirror those of his parents. The crying baby, for example, probably has a tense, inept, or upset mother. The older the child, the more his inner life and intrapsychic conflicts contribute to whatever difficulties he has.

2. The terms "infant," "child," "latency child," "adolescent," and so on, have the same validity as other diagnostic terms. They point to possible insights, but must not be taken as definitive. One must understand *this* total individual in his total situation.

3. Beware of generalizations about the needs of children. One needs to ask: What infant or what child? What age? What phase? What environmental circumstance? Granting that the infant needs unlimited mothering, this very implication of tender, loving care must also envision the gradual, tactful weaning and the imposition of limits and requirements. In the teens, again, strict limit-setting frequently gives security at thirteen or fourteen, but a progressively freer rein is probably indicated after that. One high school senior who at thirteen or so sought out a highly disciplined girls' drill team said to her parents, "You guys weren't tough enough with us." But she meant at thirteen, not at eighteen!

4. Do not avoid "harsh" diagnostic terms if they are indicated. It is no favor to a child, his family, or the community to gloss over real problems. A socially deprived child who cannot keep up in school because he has never experienced the necessary verbal or other tools is just as retarded, from an operational point of view, as a brain-damaged child. It may be possible to alleviate social deficiencies or psychological blocks through counseling, but it may be necessary simultaneously to protect the child from hopelessly competitive situations. The "harsh diagnosis," incidentally, is for your own thinking; it is not something with which to burden the client or his family. And it is always subject to revision!

1. Margaretha A. Ribble, *The Rights of Infants* (New York: Columbia University Press, 1943).

2. Mary E. Bergen, "The Effect of Severe Trauma on a Four-Year-Old Child," *Psychoanalytic Study of the Child*, 13:407–429, 1958.

3. Peter Blos, *On Adolescence: A Psychoanalytic Interpretation* (New York: The Free Press of Glencoe, 1962).

4. Gerald H. J. Pearson, *Adolescence and the Conflict of Generations* (New York: W. W. Norton & Co., Inc., 1958).

CHAPTER NINE

Personality Problems

A. *Alcoholism*

Counselors probably do not encounter many alcoholics, but they are almost certain to see their wives or other members of their families. A few words about "problem drinkers" are therefore in order. Perhaps the most important thing for the counselor is to avoid the extremes of optimism or pessimism about a so-called alcoholic. One has to know considerable about a given situation before knowing what may be therapeutically possible.

Pathological drinking usually takes one of two forms: (1) constant, almost daily abuse of alcohol resulting in more or less chronic drunkenness; or (2) episodic or periodic sprees, lasting from a few days to a few weeks, followed by remorse or even depression and variable periods of abstinence. More or less borderline conditions include (1) the not uncommon Saturday night weekend drinking that may not interfere with work but nevertheless disrupts marital or social life; and (2) constant "sipping" on the job or daily "two-hour luncheons" that are felt as necessary to keep on top of one's work and to facilitate business contacts, but which often result in self-defeat. In general, alcoholism is a "disease" when it materially interferes with an individual's domestic, vocational, or general social adjustments, or threatens to impair his health. These are usually interrelated, of course, and the total life situation is affected.

Years ago Robert P. Knight distinguished *essential* from *reactive* alcoholism. Excessive drinking in essential alcoholics is due to early and deeply rooted personality disorders. Reactive alcoholism, by contrast, does not represent a lifelong behavior pattern but is rather a way of reacting to some current stressful situation; marital conflict, loss of love object, business failure, unemployment, and so on. This division of alcoholics does not explain the problem by any means, but it has its "rule of thumb" usefulness in early diagnosis.

A complicating fact is that there are (or may be) sociocultural and physiological as well as psychological determinants. How does one explain, for example, high alcoholic rates among the Irish and Swedes, and low rates among Jews and Chinese; or, at any rate, among their descendants in the United States? From a psychodynamic point of view, it is clear that people may drink to lower their defenses ("dissolve the superego") or to strengthen their defenses, or simply to anesthetize painful conflicts. Again, from a psychiatric diagnostic point of view, an alcoholic may be a "psychopathic personality," a psychotic, a mentally retarded person, or a psychoneurotic.

These are somewhat old-fashioned terms, of course, and reflect neither the remote origins nor the current adaptive or coping attempts of the individual alcoholic.

To the extent that alcoholic tendencies can be conceptualized as to their psychological origins, we can say that they originate from experiences of oral indulgence and oral frustration early in infancy, which give rise to threats to inner security and well-being; but which, at the same time, give rise to the magical belief in a fluid (originally associated with mothering) that dispels tension, aloneness, rage, and depression, and also provides pleasure, contentment, relaxation, and increased self-esteem. In more current terms, excessive alcoholic consumption—psychologically, at least—represents an effort to counteract, and at the same time express, unbearably lonely, depressed, aggressive and, at the same time, self-destructive impulses. It is for these reasons that alcoholic addiction is, in the words of Karl Menninger, a kind of "partial suicide."

A number of very brief case résumés will indicate types of situations encountered in counseling:

Mrs. Y. presents a marital problem. She complains that her husband, who is on his fourth marriage, began drinking after failures in business. He became nervous and tremulous, started to drink too much, became depressed, and made one suicidal attempt. His excessive drinking has continued. Mrs. Y. has learned that her husband was divorced by all three of his previous wives and that he has been involved in scandal that he has never revealed to her. Mrs. Y. is herself obviously a compulsive neurotic. She has always worked excessively hard, married late, and now spends eighteen to twenty hours a day keeping her small home clean. She is hypochondriacal, a chronic worrier, and has been seen to smile only twice in the two years she has been known to the counselor. The evidence suggests that the marital situation involves a very neurotic wife and a husband who is a reactive alcoholic. Although never too stable, he nevertheless achieved considerable success prior to his marriage to Mrs. Y., and drank pathologically only after a former wife involved him in a scandal which ruined his business.

Mrs. I., a twenty-five-year-old widow with three preschool children, comes for assistance a few weeks after the suicide of her husband. She dates the onset of her difficulties to a time, some five years previously and three weeks after her marriage, when she learned that her husband had asthma, a fact he had neglected to tell her. The record says: "She remained with him but never recovered from her feeling of betrayal by him." Their first child, born a year later, was wanted by her but unwanted by her husband. The other two children were unplanned. After the first year or so of marriage. the husband drank to excess, gambled, and lost various jobs, so that the family had to live with her parents. The husband's drinking increased, Mrs. I. finally determined to sue for divorce, and the husband then committed suicide. Mrs. I.'s mother-in-law blamed her for the suicide. In this case we know little about the husband, but again we have a somewhat neurotic or infantile wife who cannot recover from not having been told that her husband has asthma. The husband's drinking, if it did not spring from a severe personality disorder, may well have been in part reactive to rejection and frustration by Mrs. I.

Mr. S. drank constantly and to excess. After each "spree" he would discuss his problems very freely with the worker, always bringing up the subject himself and insisting that in reality he could "leave the stuff alone." He always blamed his lapses from sobriety on his common-law wife, since he only got drunk after an episode or period of infidelity on her part. This, despite the client's story, is more "essential" than "reactive" drinking, and prospects for change with counseling are dim.

Miss B., a twenty-eight-year-old unmarried girl, has been seeing a psychiatrist, but cannot afford further consultations and is referred to a family agency. Her problem involves great hostility toward her parents and parent-surrogates, but inability to break away from them. From the psychiatrist's and also from the client's material, it is evident that the client has been rejected by her parents, both of whom are chronic alcoholics, since she became adolescent, if not before. The problem is essentially that of a severely neurotic girl, but the parents' emotional difficulties, expressed in part in chronic alcoholism, form the background of the client's maladjustment.

Treatment of alcoholics will not usually fall to the counselor. Essential alcoholism, in particular, is a psychiatric problem. It is almost impossible to treat outside an institution, and the prognosis even with treatment must be guarded. It may be stated flatly that, for the chronic alcoholic, there can be no compromise with liquor; he has to "go on the wagon" 100 per cent. He may benefit from insight into the psychodynamics of his illness through psychotherapy or psychoanalysis, and from association with such groups of reformed alcoholics as "Alcoholics Anonymous." Many of the "quick cures" for alcoholism make no pretense of preventing relapses, but several attempt to build up a "conditioned response" against liquor in all forms. The whole subject of therapy for alcoholics lacks clarity because of inadequate follow-up studies and failure to agree on a classification of types of pathological drinkers.

The counselor may encounter situations, especially involving reactive alcoholism, in which manipulation of the external environment or relief of emotional tensions through interviews may so relieve an individual's total situation as to enable him to give up pathological drinking. Certainly it is within the province of a counselor to alleviate economic distress, marital discord, and other such problems, of which reactive alcoholism may be symptomatic. The closer a given case approaches essential alcoholism, however, the less chance the counselor has of getting therapeutic results from the tools at his command, and he may save himself a good deal of heartbreak and waste of time if he will drop most such clients from his case load.

As has been stated, the practical problem for the counselor in evaluating alcoholism is the matter of severity. One important diagnostic clue is that of chronicity. Has the client been drinking heavily for years or is this difficulty of recent onset? Related to this is the relative importance of genetic and "vertical" determinants as contrasted to situational or "horizontal" factors. Generally speaking, the outlook for a favorable response to counseling is good where horizontal factors predominate; i.e., where excessive drinking is mostly the result of recent or current environmental stresses.

In those clients whose excessive drinking is not clearly a result of current situational or environmental problems, it is best to regard the alcoholism as, essentially, a psychiatric problem. This does not mean that the client must be referred to a psychiatrist, but rather that a more definitive diagnosis is called for. If the drinking represents a neurotic compulsion to defeat or otherwise punish the client, then psychoanalysis is probably the treatment of choice, possibly in a psychiatric hospital setting. If a latent depression or schizophrenia is masked by the alcoholism, it is important not to take away the defense without treating what lies behind it. If, again, alcoholism expresses a long-standing personality problem, then a "total push" treatment program may well be indicated: counseling, Alcoholics Anonymous, and treatment of the spouse or parents. The article on "Alcoholism" in the *Encyclopedia of Mental Health* is an excellent review of the practical problems of and solutions for the alcoholic who has really lost control of his use of alcohol.

B. *Depressions*

Depressions are disturbances of mood, primarily, in which one is sad, "blue," dejected, slowed down, and generally uninterested in life. In severe depressions there are feelings of guilt, self-accusations of sin or wasted opportunities, signs of agitation, and near immobilization of interests and activities. Suicidal preoccupation may or may not be expressed openly. In the most severe cases of depression—not often seen by a counselor—evidence of thought disorders also appear, a psychotic "break with reality." In addition, the patient may have regressed to the point of wetting and soiling himself and, like a helpless infant, may require total care if he is to survive.

Depression may be masked in various ways. Boredom and apathy are examples; alcoholism is another. "Drivenness" of one sort or another—overwork, overplay, "over" almost anything—may represent efforts to prevent or ward off feelings of depression. Neurotic invalidism or hypochondria are still other ways of defending against depression.

Depressive states have in common a loss of self-esteem which is felt, unconsciously, as a loss of love. There may be an actual loss—such as the death of a parent, spouse, or child, or the loss of important other supplies for self-esteem, money, home, looks, career, reputation, etc.—or the loss may be more in terms of inner wishes, demands, or expectations. The dynamics of depression are such that there are two principal reactions: (1) "I don't deserve to live"; and (2) "Life isn't worth living." In the first instance the guilt and aggression are turned primarily toward the self; in the second, the person or Fate held responsible is outside the self. If these feelings are intense and prolonged enough, suicide may occur.

The depression that follows a death or other loss is known as mourning so long as it follows the usual and normal course accepted by a given culture. People are expected to recover from any severe loss in a few weeks or months, and if they do not one begins to substitute *depression* for *mourning*. It then becomes important to look for other situational factors, beyond the recent death, as well as intrapsychic factors such as guilt over earlier death wishes toward the deceased, frustrated dependency wishes, and the like.

Here are examples of depressive reactions: Infants, for example, show all of the external signs of depression (whatever they may feel) if they lack mothering; i.e., being held, rocked, played with, and otherwise given close physical and verbal recognition. René Spitz, for example, described pictures of marked apathy, listlessness, and depressed facial expression in infants left by their mothers at about six months of age, and in other infants and young children living in hospitals or orphanages for long periods. The story was told, some years ago, of an ultramodern children's hospital that had everything for its young patients, but where the children, nevertheless, were doing poorly. Finally, someone made the needed diagnosis and, for each child, prescribed: "To be picked up and mothered, one-half hour twice a day."

Apparent depressive reactions can be noted in much less drastic circumstances. A boy of two and a half whose father had played with him daily, seemed to be depressed for some weeks after the father left home for military duty. He could not express what he felt, but changes in eating, toilet habits, and facial expression *suggested* depression.

Older children may react in similar fashion to family separations for various reasons—military service, hospitalization, divorce, or death—with such symptoms, plus verbalized expressions of loss of interest, apathy, hopelessness, or resentment.

Parenthetically, it is perhaps worth pointing out that all of us—in theory, at least—emerge from childhood with a depressive or a paranoid predisposition; i.e., a tendency to feel responsibility and guilt for our suffering (hence, depressive) or a tendency to project the responsibility and to blame others, or Fate (hence, paranoid). It would be more accurate, perhaps, to suggest that all of us emerge from childhood having had experiences of separation, deprivation, and loss. Accordingly, we have all suffered depression of greater or less intensity. If, then, we assume that these experiences have occurred because we were bad and that we are responsible, the related feelings are those of guilt, shame, remorse, and further depression. We feel that we are not only alienated from others but also from ourselves.

If we do not accept responsibility, but project it, then we can blame others: family, friends, Jews, Communists, God, or Fate. This does not preclude depression, however. Paranoid individuals are often in acute conflict about current substitutes for past objects that have been lost. They are persnickety about food and drink, and they are pathologically jealous about friends, lovers, and spouses. Many are alcoholic or near-alcoholic. From this point of view, then, paranoid conditions may simply represent attempts to deal with depression by projective devices; otherwise the principal symptoms are an expression of turning against oneself.

To be more accurate, it is the anger, aggression, and vindictiveness connected with a loss, a deprivation, or a hurt that may be handled in these ways. When we are weaned, when Mother goes away, when a brother or sister is born, we suffer a sense of loss, deprivation, hurt, and rage. It is the manner in which we deal with the rage and the wish to get even that is frequently the principal force behind our defensive operations.

Depressive reactions in adolescents (*and* adults) sometimes occur when they do not or cannot achieve their goals. The level of aspiration is frequently much higher than the level of performance or achievement. When one feels that he has failed his parents, his friends, his teachers, or his own conscience, the sense of failure may create depression. The goal is equated (unconsciously, at least) with parental acceptance and love, and failure to attain it, with disapproval and rejection. The resulting loss of self-esteem is tantamount to feeling, "If I cannot do whatever it takes—or whatever I *imagine* it takes—to please my parents, then I am a failure and life is not worth living." Also, even more unconsciously (if that is possible), "And, besides, they are bad, wicked parents for demanding so much of me, and I hate them and I hope that my failure will make them rue the day they attached such conditions to loving me."

Such depressive reactions are conspicuous in highly competitive situations. They occur in (apparently) trivial circumstances such as the inability of a boy to "make the team," of a girl to "get into the right sorority," or of a man to get a certain job. With the increasing importance of high school and higher education, both school and parental pressures increase to the point that both internal and external factors make failures take on catastrophic proportions. We in the United States are approaching the situation of English and Continental education where, at the age of thirteen or so, the die is cast as to whether one becomes a professional man or a clerk, a technician, or an unskilled laborer. The competition has become so keen and, in a sense, so deadly that college (and even high school) is no longer fun—except for the most gifted—but, on the contrary, is frequently a mad, harrowing struggle for survival. It is out of educational, vocational, and professional situations like these that counselors receive many clients with depressive and other serious "stress reactions."

Severe depression may be suspected when the client is withdrawn, listless, uncommunicative, and slow in movements and responses. This "psychomotor retardation" must alert the counselor, however reluctantly, to the possibility that the client is suicidal. It is a signal for the counselor to pursue the matter tactfully but actively. If direct questions about how things are going are shrugged off, then ask the client if he feels "blue" or "low in spirits." He may agree that "things look pretty hopeless" or that he "might as well be dead."

If the client will reveal this much of his mood, the matter can safely be probed a little further. Does he have suicidal thoughts? He probably has. Has he thought of ways of ending it all? Maybe he has and maybe he has not. If he has, has he actually taken any steps? If it turns out that the client has, indeed, accumulated sleeping pills, or loaded a revolver, or made any other actual preparations, then the chance of suicide is great. Psychiatric referral is indicated in any case; but evidence of definite preparation creates an emergency. The counselor must disregard the client's protestations and with all firmness insist that the client be seen by a psychiatrist or taken to a hospital. Despite angry or tearful protestations about unworthiness or disgrace, the client will usually be relieved and, in the long run, grateful.

These are intensely unpleasant situations for a counselor, and he needs to remember his own resistance to them. He would prefer not to think that a client of his would really commit suicide. He would prefer to avoid asking the difficult questions that establish the facts, and taking steps that the client overtly opposes. But the steps must be taken, and all of the kind firmness the counselor can muster is indicated.

There are several rules of thumb about suicidal risks. One is that a person in the depths of a depression—a very severe depression, that is—is less likely to commit suicide than later on, when he starts to "come out of it." When he is immobilized by depression, he simply lacks the energy to exert himself; later, as the psychomotor paralysis lessens, he may make the attempt.

Another "rule" is, of course, that a person does not have to be depressed to commit suicide. At least, the depression does not have to show. People who feel terribly rejected may murder, or they may commit suicide. Here the principal affect is fury. The underlying dynamics are depressive, no doubt; i.e., they involve a murderous attack against an introjected object, following an acute or chronic loss of self-esteem. The more overt reasons, however, include chronic illness and pain, loneliness, rejections by a love object, loss of whatever confers status and prestige, and actual or impending disgrace.

A recent study of a series of psychiatric patients who attempted suicide while driving cars revealed that (out of thirty) only one had a psychotic depression. One had a "mixed psychosis," and four were schizophrenic. The remaining twenty-four were considered to have hysterical, passive-aggressive, and sociopathic or other personality disorders. Depression, where present, was fleeting and not (openly) profound. In one half of the series, the suicidal attempt was impulsive and followed an argument with a lover, spouse, neighbor, or boss.

A certain proportion of suicides occurs among persons of any age who have been living under conditions of loneliness and despair. They have neither friends nor relatives; and poor health, poor jobs, unemployment, discrimination, or other conditions of life generate feelings of hopelessness. "Crisis clinics" are springing up as a resource for such persons. The motto is, in effect, "Call us instead of doing violence to yourself." Such twenty-four-hour-a-day resources should be invaluable in any community that can sustain them. They are finding, however, that the appeals for help are endless, and by no means restricted to the desperate. They are finding, too, that "love is not enough"; i.e., that while relationship and friendliness will provide a social cure for some, a great deal more is required—definitive treatment, that is—for others.

C. *Sexual Perversions*

Counselors may not see many persons who suffer from sexual perversions. One reason is that they seldom experience overt suffering. They come only after they have been caught, and the principal help they want is in avoiding prosecution. Treatment, therefore, is treatment in an authoritative setting.

If this sounds harsh, it is nevertheless true of a majority. Sigmund Freud once said that neurosis is the opposite of perversion. Part of what he meant by this is that in the cases of neurosis, it is the neurotic individual who suffers; in the case of perversion, it is others. The principal anxiety of most perverse individuals is social anxiety; i.e., that of being detected and punished.

By definition, sexual perversions include all forms of sexual gratification that are not commonly considered part of normal heterosexual intercourse. The concept of "normal" is somewhat fluid, of course, but it excludes incest, or taking a child as a sexual object, or a person of the same sex, or an animal. It also rules out "peeping," exhibitionism (except when sublimated), and other interests and activities that young children are generally trained to give up and to regard as bad, dirty, or forbidden. Many "perverse" activities are not so regarded if they lead to and culminate in heterosexual, genital intercourse, but are considered perverse if they remain ends in themselves. From another point of view, whatever deviates from cultural norms is perverse.

A high school girl came to interview a psychiatrist about psychiatry as a career—this was an assignment!— and in the course of the conversation brought out the fact that she had recently been the victim of an exhibitionist. She seemed quite poised and mature about the whole episode, but she wondered at the same time about the fact that her first reaction was one of intense fury: for a moment she wanted to murder the man. The psychiatrist, recalling that this was an assigned interview, simply remarked that such feelings were not surprising to him; after all, he added, this was an invasion of her privacy, a forced intimacy, and a kind of psychic rape.

There may well have been other determinants. Had the girl come for counseling because she was upset for days or weeks after the experience, she might have had to explore more complicated feelings. She might unconsciously have invited the episode or, if not, at least enjoyed it, but only with a sense of shame and guilt. The rage, again, might in part express "castrating impulses" toward boys and men in general, and the shock consisted in these impulses becoming so obvious to her. In any case the problem with the object of a pervert is not merely "What did you feel?" but, more, "How many things did you feel?"

This is, of course, the difficulty with little girls who are sexually fondled by old men. Here, too, in a surprising number of instances, it takes two to make a seduction. It does not excuse the adult, to be sure, but the fact remains that little girls are frequently very seductive, sometimes quite consciously so. And it is not uncommonly part of the child's subsequent emotional problem that she actively wanted or at least passively enjoyed the experience. Someone once made a follow-up study of girls who had been "molested" as young children and discovered that most of them, when not too much to-do had been made of the episode at the time, had made quite happy marriages. Whether a child is "ruined for life" by the sexual experiences of childhood will depend to a considerable extent on how the grown-ups react at the time.

Homosexuality is an extremely complicated personal and social problem because, on the one hand, it is a crime and yet, on the other, it can be ostensibly a normal way of life. A large number of psychiatrists view homosexuality as a kind of arrested psychosexual development and the homosexual as an immature individual who, because of mixed-up identifications or deep neurotic fears, is incapable of forming enduring heterosexual attachments leading to marriage and parenthood. Even this is an oversimplification, however, because some homosexuals marry and have children, and it is such persons, or members of their families, who are most likely to ask for help.

The counselor who is called upon to work with homosexuals, those who are otherwise sexually deviate, their victims, or their relatives should try to remember the following: (1) these behaviors are normal in very young children; (2) they can be within normal limits in older children, including early teen-agers; (3) they can be one-time episodes in adolescence and, indeed, at any age; (4) they may be symptomatic of neurosis, and therefore psychoanalytically treatable; (5) they may represent faulty character or personality development, and therefore be very difficult, if not impossible, to treat. Other things being equal, the younger the individual and the greater the intrapsychic conflict, the better the outlook with treatment.

The counselor will discover, however, that many homosexuals are content with their mode of life and do not wish to change. They wish protection from social condemnation and from laws that make a crime of homosexuality. They tend to idealize their kind of adjustment and would like to have it accepted as normal. The difficulty with this, however, is that most homosexuals are very promiscuous; there are few stable and enduring relationships among them. Psychologically speaking, there is intense hostility behind the homosexual facade of many, and their relationships are strikingly sadomasochistic. It would be better to regard homosexuality and other perversions as forms of maladaptation rather than crimes, recognizing at the same time that the community needs protection from their manifestations just as it does, for example, from the tuberculous.

A young adolescent exhibitionist was sent to Juvenile Court on complaint of a neighbor. The court sent the boy to a psychiatrist who found that he was living in an otherwise female household. The exhibitionism seemed to be an angry assertion of his masculinity which the boy felt was being depreciated and submerged. Arrangements were made for more masculine contacts and activities, and some years later it appeared that the exhibitionism had been successfully shunted off into public speaking.

A gloomier picture is revealed by most studies of the sexually deviate. From a psychiatric point of view, they are not a homogeneous diagnostic group. On the contrary, the perverse behavior may be part of the symptomatic picture of psychoses, psychoneuroses, intoxicated states, "psychopathic pesonalities," organic brain diseases, or mental deficiencies.

It is true, again, that there is little neurotic suffering in most cases of perversion. When apprehended by the police, "perverts" vehemently deny the charges, inventing all sorts of excuses; e.g., an overwhelming need to urinate as a reason for exposure. Even when treatment is offered, some prefer to stand trial. Many of those who do accept the offer of treatment drop out as soon as legal charges are withdrawn. The incentive is more the threat of punishment than of intrapsychic suffering. Walter Bromberg has pointed out, however, that warm, maternal women therapists may have success where others fail with sexually deviant clients.

D. *"Psychopaths"*

To call a client a psychopath is about the same as calling him a bastard. Both terms have some small claim to diagnostic precision, but they all too easily become epithets. It is somewhat the same as with the term "acting out," which frequently means any kind of behavior of which *we* do not approve. Nevertheless, so-called psychopaths or sociopaths are coming in increasing numbers to counselors—particularly to those working in social agencies—and so they are to be reckoned with. This is the more so because psychiatric clinics sometimes screen them out as untreatable.

Psychopathic or sociopathic disorders are distinguished, by psychiatrists, from the neuroses, the psychoses, the various psychosomatic conditions, and from all conditions that are secondary to impairment of brain functions due to definite organic disease. They are currently classified as "psychologically determined personality disorders." Among the personality disorders proper are, for example, inadequate personalities, schizoid personalities, and passive-aggressive personalities. The sociopathic personalities, by contrast, are those that are characterized by conspicuous antisocial or dyssocial behavior, including sexual deviations and alcoholic as well as other drug addictions.

The principal reasons for psychopathic or sociopathic behavior, in the absence of organic brain defect or disease, is faulty character or personality formation. From a psychoanalytic point of view, the superego is weak or corrupt or, on the contrary, is so dreadfully punitive that it is felt as an alien force to be eternally defied and rebelled against. Or, as sometimes seems to be the case, the drives are so strong and the repressive superego is so strong, that there is very little ego. Behavior may therefore display the ascendency of impulse or of (unconscious) remorse and guilt. In any case, the individual behaves as if he had no internal controls and is principally in conflict with the social group in which he lives.

With something like the above as a background, the psychopathic personality is impulsive, irresponsible, and unpredictable, revealing weak emotional controls and poor social adaptation. It is as if he lives selfishly, according to the "pleasure principle." Such a person appears to be unable to anticipate the consequences of his behavior or to learn from experience. He may often be described as "impulse ridden." Again, there is frequently no awareness and little indication of intrapsychic pain. What suffering the "psychopath" suffers is from his conflicts with society. Guilt may be inferred from behavior that "begs for punishment." The behavior itself is not diagnostic, of course; but when the term "psychopath" is applied, the behavior represents a severe personality disorder, not, for example, a psychosis or mental deficiency.

Some of these phenomena, if not the full dynamics, are best illustrated in brief case records: [1]

A thirty-three-year-old man came into a sanitarium because of frequent alcoholic periods in which he became violently aggressive and destructive. History revealed a powerful, domineering father and a weak, neurotic mother who kept the patient in his baby carriage until he was able to climb out by himself and in infants' dresses until the age of five. A weak, frail, only child, the patient developed into a tall and physically formidable adult. In early adult life he began drinking to excess, often wrecked his car or hotel furniture, was abusive of women friends, and got into fist fights with men. He stole money from a bank on one occasion, but was able to cover up his theft. Several engagements and one marriage went on the rocks after brief periods. It was clear that the patient's drinking was related in part to a fixation at the oral level of development and that his extreme destructiveness while drunk was in a large measure directed toward his mother or mother-figures. Guilt, self-punishment, and unconscious homosexual conflicts were also conspicuous.

A nineteen-year-old college student was hospitalized for treatment because of chronic defiance of his parents, constant preoccupation with gambling, and forging his father's name to a number of checks. The patient was precocious, ingratiating, facile, and generally charming to women, but unreliable and unpredictable. There was little evidence of conflict or guilt. His principal ambition in life appeared to be to get a million dollars by any possible means. He felt rejected and held down by his parents, and recalled early childhood experiences revealing a sense of being abandoned and rejected in favor of an elder sister.

A sixteen-year-old girl came to the attention of a Juvenile Court because of frequent stealing and running away from home. Her mother complained that she was impudent and unmanageable, stealing and cutting up her clothing. In school she was provocative and rebellious. The caseworker found her docile, demanding, and infantile. She apparently feigned illness to shirk responsibility. Her provocative behavior seemed rather to attract attention than to evoke punishment. Her IQ was found to be borderline. The patient's early family life had been marked by insecurity and this, coupled with her somewhat limited intelligence, was considered to have stunted her ego development.

A forty-year-old married woman had a city-wide reputation for "hysterical spells." Whenever frustrated by her husband or by social agencies, with which she had many dealings, she would "fall down in a convulsion" on the street thus demanding the services of the police, fire department pulmotor squad, and ambulances. She kept a file of her clippings—the newspaper accounts of these episodes. She neglected her children, but managed to make headlines when the Juvenile Court attempted to remove the younger children from the home. She was careless, improvident, and generally unstable, a "hysterical personality."

A thirty-two-year-old man came to a social agency asking for psychiatric service because of inability to hold jobs. History revealed a long story of instability, but the principal findings lay in the client's ability to hedge every request about with so many impossible restrictions and demands that it was quite impossible to work with him. The history included several arrests, difficulties about citizenship, marriage for six months without sexual intercourse, an account of having written a play calling for an urgent trip to New York to see his agent, and numerous temper tantrums and periods of depression since his marriage. Review of many pages of history gave evidence of feminine identification, sexual immaturity, masturbation after marriage, unreliability, incapacity for sustained work or interest, escape from responsibility through illness, and a host of other neurotic, psychosomatic, and disordered personality traits.

Ruthless psychiatrists, in the past, have suggested that such personalities should be dumped together on an otherwise deserted island, and allowed to fight it out. William Golding's *The Lord of the Flies* [2] suggests vividly what the outcome might be. On the other hand, something like this was done by August Aichhorn [3] with a group of delinquent boys, but the highly important difference was that understanding and treatment were available when the boys came to the point of accepting them. Anyone who works with these people must have the patience of Job, and even then he must expect nothing to happen with a large proportion.

To the extent that psychopathic behavior becomes delinquent or criminal behavior, institutional treatment becomes inevitable. If the individual so affected comes to a counselor before he is legally confined—or because he is "given another chance"—he should, if possible, be placed in a restricted, carefully supervised environment where he can simultaneously have psychiatric or related intensive therapy.

This will protect him, as well as society, from his own behavior. There is no reason for an attitude of therapeutic nihilism if the client is young; if he can be made aware of some sense of responsibility and wish to change; and if favorable environmental therapy can be provided, together with insight therapy and the opportunity for strengthening healthy identifications. These are rather big "ifs," perhaps, but the counselor will avoid despair if he remembers that "love is not enough" in some of these cases; or, rather, that love, like that for a very young child, includes discipline: justice, firmness, setting limits to impulsive behavior, opportunity for healthy emotional attachments, and strengthening of normal ego defenses and controls.

E. *Other Personality Problems*

Counselors trained some years ago may wonder what has become of "neurotic characters" and "character disorders." There is no consensus as yet, but the tendency is to get away from a separation of "character" from the total personality. Most classifications now describe a number of "personality disorders" or "personality reactions." The terms "character traits" and "personality traits" may be used interchangeably, and likewise such descriptive terms as "hysterical character" and "hysterical personality" or "inhibited character" and "inhibited personality." Neither Karl Menninger in *The Vital Balance* nor the most recent American Medical Association *Current Medical Terminology* makes use of the characterological terminology.

What we are concerned with, in any case, are types of overdevelopment, underdevelopment, or distorted development of personality traits which otherwise, if within normal limits, make for flexible and yet harmonious living in social groups. By almost any definition of personal and social maturity, one must be able to give as well as to receive. To a considerable extent, one must be able to put away childish things, but still understand them. Sexuality and aggression must be curbed, must not be expressed perversely, but must not be totally inhibited or suppressed. All counselors have certain working conceptions as to what behaviors are within normal limits and what are not. "Personality problems" are part of an attempt to designate some of the behaviors that are not.

The cases that most frequently perplex counselors, perhaps, are clients who are conspicuously adequate in most respects, but whose pregenital (oral, narcissistic, anal, or hysterical) personality traits—inadequately subordinated or integrated—are a source of misery to themselves or others. The problems are the greater because they are hidden behind a facade of charm, intelligence, and accomplishment. The counselor, impressed by the client's obvious ego strengths, forgets that these, at times, cannot make up for other weaknesses. If adequacy is a defense against repressed dependency, for example, it will be difficult to use the former to combat symptoms of the latter, or even of the conflict between them.

A college graduate working successfully as a research assistant came for counseling because of feelings of inadequacy and depression. Although quite attractive and intelligent, she felt inferior. Despite explicit reassurance from her boss, she felt she would be fired. As counseling progressed, her interpersonal relations were revealed as shallow, tenuous, and sexually promiscuous. She tended to have the opinions and values of the person she was closest to at the moment. Her early family life had included separation of her parents and the death of one of them when she was still a child.

With such information and other data her difficulties clearly included regressive defenses against separation anxiety and Oedipal guilt combined with arrested ego development in important affective spheres. One brief schizophrenic episode, carefully concealed from everyone but the counselor, indicated the fragility of her defenses but was also a healing experience: The voice of God himself had provided her with solutions.

What to call her? Oral, narcissistic, schizoid, hysterical, paranoid, depressive personality. Any or all of these would indicate the truth, but not the whole truth. The point here is that no one seeing her on the street would see more than a good-looking, well-dressed, apparently intelligent young woman, and few with whom she worked would add much more except that she was chatty but often moody and remote. Even the counselor was astonished that so much pathology could lie behind so much apparent ego strength.

A sixty-five-year-old widow provided a comparable surprise. She came for help because of a male tenant of whom she wanted to be rid. It soon appeared that her feelings about this man were very mixed, and equally so about the rather large house in which they lived. At first glance this was a largely situational problem confronting an older woman left alone with her home and ample funds.

As the relationship developed, however, there was no solution. The client could neither accept the man nor get rid of him. She was unable to decide about the house. There was something wrong about her outside life and social relationships. She manipulated people and played them off against each other. When it was possible to reconstruct her life history her behavior made more sense. It could be seen that lifelong defenses were crumbling with advancing age, and she was increasingly threatened by potential dependency.

The story, in brief, was that she lost both parents when she was very young and dealt with the subsequent vicissitudes by defenses of exaggerated independence and adequacy. Her personality was marked by reaction formations against hostility and dependent needs, and her sexual relationships were with depreciated and inadequate men. She easily became overly involved with those who needed her. She completed college and had postgraduate work. She had been a successful professional woman for thirty years.

Her personal relationships betrayed her defensive adjustment, marked as it was by conspicuous ego strengths. Her professional life provided her with dozens of immature persons who feared her, needed her, looked up to her, and idealized her. Her first husband was alcoholic and unfaithful, and she supported him for most of fifteen married years. Her second marriage was more satisfactory, but for the first three years she grieved for the husband whom she had just divorced. When the second husband died, she took into her home the man she later wanted to expel. He was generous and helpful, but he got drunk and was a problem. They needed each other, but it was mostly she who could not admit the need. Her failure to get rid of him was on the basis that she "felt sorry for him." The situation, in a word, was that this woman's habitual independence and self-sufficiency were becoming unrealistic for her actual situation and that as these defenses ceased to serve her, she was threatened once more with all of the turmoil of early childhood, related to loss, separation, and death. The personality problems of decades had been masked by a successful professional career, but the mask was beginning to fall away.

Such clients need support and sometimes firm direction. Their old defenses can frequently be bolstered by activities similar to the careers they have had to leave behind. It often helps for them to lead ritualistic lives and to find ways of "doing for others" in whatever capacities are appropriate to their actual capabilities. This has been called "reinstating compulsive defenses," and it may be more effective than clarification or interpretation or other efforts to effect some basic change.

F. *Schizophrenics*

Schizophrenia is another of those "scare words" the use of which Karl Menninger, among others, has long deplored. In any case, most psychiatrists have long since stopped talking about "schizophrenia" and refer, instead, to "the schizophrenias." Others—not many!—have dealt with the problem by claiming that "everybody is schizophrenic." This is true enough, of course, if one looks at one's dreams and fantasies, but it is about as definitive as stating that everyone is human.

The schizophrenias, generally speaking, may be considered psychologically determined, relatively severe emotional disorders that usually have their overt onset early in life; i.e., adolescence or young adulthood. Characteristically, they are marked by withdrawal from reality; stilted or emotionless interpersonal relationships; bizarre or at least paradoxical emotional and intellectual responses; and, in the more transparently sick, varying degrees of regression from slight silliness to unmistakable manifestations of delusions and hallucinations. In other words, if one is to speak of the schizophrenias at all, one has to recognize that while they are primarily "thought disorders" and disturbances in interpersonal relationships with variable regression and withdrawal from reality, they do nevertheless differ considerably in their outward manifestations and in the degree of seriousness from the point of view of adaptive capacities.

The point of this is that there are many persons who are, or have been, schizophrenic and for whom a counselor can do much. Diagnostically, the individual may be tabbed as a latent schizophrenic, a recovered schizophrenic, a schizophrenic in remission, or simply an extremely schizoid person. He may, in other words, be an isolate, an extremely lonely person, an individual who can hold a job and otherwise cope with life, but have few, if any, friendships or close ties of any sort. He may be a migrant, a highly educated person in a menial job, a back-in-the-stacks librarian, a schoolteacher, or a career research person. Such people tend to have solitary jobs with minimal supervision, and to live solitary lives otherwise. This is not what they prefer, really, but it is what they can tolerate.

Some clients of this general type simply want the counselor "to be there." They want to be able to come around and "check in" from time to time. It is as if they need to feel that someone is interested and concerned, even though the meetings are infrequent. They do not want probing or intensive counseling or even too much demonstrative concern; they do want a relationship, but mostly on their terms. This is supportive treatment for those who need it this way, and the relationship may last for years. The counselor needs mostly to know that this *is* enough for these clients, and that they require plenty of notice if there is to be a change.

Other schizoid or mildly schizophrenic clients will do better if the counselor assumes a somewhat parental role.

A combination of making suggestions, giving advice, and environmental manipulation may keep the client from making damaging mistakes and, at the same time, foster a better social and vocational adjustment. Group therapy may be a helpful adjunct to individual counseling, partly because it is a social experience. The counselor should not hesitate to use praise and encouragement in connection with actual efforts and accomplishments, but should avoid the trap of therapeutic ambition or putting the achievement ahead of the person.

A colleague once asked about a therapist to whom a famous artist might be referred. A name was suggested with the added comment, "He is particularly interested in the creative process." The colleague retorted, "That would be fatal. My patient wants someone to be interested in him, not in his art!" The point was well taken, and a possible mistake in referral was thereby averted. This happened to be a very schizoid artist, but the moral is clear whatever the diagnosis.

G. *Counseling in Industry*

Counseling in industry is counseling in a particular setting. It is mentioned here simply because many of the problems just discussed come to light on the job. The overt problem may be absenteeism, inefficiency, accident proneness, withdrawal from others, or frequent conflicts with fellow employees, subordinates, or superiors. Often enough, however, such problems are symptomatic of others, including sickness at home, worry over finances, difficulty with children, marital conflict, or long-standing personality maladjustment of one sort or another. Dr. Harry Levinson of the Menninger Foundation has written *Emotional Health in the World of Work*,[4] and the reader is referred to this as an excellent resource for counselors in general as well as personnel people and executives in business and industry.

1. For longer, vividly described case histories see Cleckley, Hervey, *The Mask of Sanity* (St. Louis: C. V. Mosby Co., 1941).

2. William Golding, *The Lord of the Flies*, Capricorn Books (New York: G. P. Putnam's Sons, 1959).

3. August Aichhorn, *Wayward Youth* (New York: The Viking Press, 1936).

4. Harry Levinson, *Emotional Health in the World of Work* (New York: Harper & Row, 1964).

CHAPTER TEN

Psychosomatic Problems

Psychosomatic is a dirty word among the elite, but it is so well established in the language as to be unavoidable. The individual man, woman, or child is a total personality living in and interacting with a total environment, and it is no more possible to isolate the psychosomatic aspects of behavior than the psychosocial. For practical purposes, as we have seen, it is nevertheless useful to emphasize one or another aspect of the total Gestalt and so, at times, we artificially separate out the physical, the social, the psychological, or the interpersonal. The psychosomatic *point of view*, then, refers to particular ways of looking at relationships between two aspects of the whole.

The concept of multiple causation holds for sickness just as it does for other behaviors. We must therefore avoid the implication that emotions (alone) cause ulcers or hypertension. Nevertheless there is a useful psychosomatic point of view. It has been outlined by Milton Rosenbaum and Morton F. Reiser somewhat as follows: [1]

The sick *patient*, rather than the *disease process* itself, is the key to understanding the illness.

It recognizes the interaction of physiological and

psychological forces in *two* directions. On the one hand, emotional tensions can be one of the causative elements of physical illness; on the other, physical illnesses, disruptive as they often are, produce psychological sequelae that may be very significant in the total clinical picture encountered by the physician or other counselor.

It is an approach that attempts to apply the best and most complete psychodynamic understanding of human personality functioning from the relevant contributions of all behavioral sciences to diagnosis, treatment, and research.

It recognizes the doctor-patient and the counselor-client relationships to be two-way interpersonal reaction systems. It pays explicit attention to the psychological participation of both as pertinent factors in both understanding and influencing the course of therapy. As applied to medical practice, therefore, it accentuates the role of doctor as counselor!

With these considerations stated, we may use the now familiar vocabulary.

A. *Common Psychosomatic Manifestations*

So-called physical manifestations of emotional states are frequently encountered in everyday life. One is embarrassed; one blushes. The blush depends upon a sudden filling of capillary vessels in the face and neck with warm, red blood; more than is usually present. Behind the blush is some emotion: embarrassment, anger, guilt. A person gets bad news at dinnertime; he "loses his appetite" or may even vomit. The success of the so-called "Lie Detector" depends upon reading the objectively measurable changes in pulse rate, rate of respiration, and blood pressure in response to strong emotions (fear, guilt) when the "dangerous question" is asked.

Similar responses affect various functions of the body. A schoolboy, worried about an impending examination, may urinate more frequently than usual. Menstruation is often suppressed entirely during periods of emotional stress. The secretion of hydrochloric acid in the stomach may be increased markedly by anxiety or other emotional states. A physician friend told this story on himself:

Because of cancer of the rectum, he had a colostomy which, of course, exposed some of the mucous membrane that lines the large bowel. One day he took a phone call in the bathroom while he was cleaning the colostomy. The call was from an angry woman patient whom he attempted to appease and placate without becoming angry himself. As he absorbed her punishing words, however, he noted the mucosa of the colostomy: it was becoming dotted, minute by minute, with tiny hemorrhagic spots or, as he called them, petechiae. He assumed that they were a response to his otherwise unexpressed feelings toward his patient.

The following cases were reported by Drs. Bela Mittelmann and Harold G. Wolff of New York: [2]

A thirty-year-old man was shocked when a fellow worker dropped dead of a heart attack. He began to have "heartburn" himself. He did not confide his trouble to his wife, and it grew worse . . . his stomach acid rose 167 per cent.

A forty-five-year-old man who had been ousted from home by his family and jailed for stealing; was living meagerly on relief; his pride had been wounded by a hospital doorman who refused to let him use the visitors' entrance. On airing his tribulations his stomach acid first dropped, then rose, reaching a peak when his anger was manifestly greatest. Bloody shreds and bile were also found in the specimens.

A sixty-year-old man with duodenal ("peptic") ulcer who had married a servant girl and was on bad terms with her was having an affair with another servant. He felt that his standing in the community, once high, was crumbling. When he was tested . . . his acid flow was quadrupled.

These cases, especially the second, might have appeared among the clients of any counselor. Two other aspect of the interrelationship between psychological tensions and physical changes are not brought out in these cases: (1) that what begins as a physiological disturbance of function, such as excess secretion of acid in the stomach, may after a period of time contribute to a definite organic structural change, as an ulcer; and (2) that different *unconscious* emotions (anxiety, anger, and so on) may bring about the same physiological changes. In the second case the gastric acidity was highest when the man's anger was *manifestly* greatest; with other people, however, the same symptoms occur without overt experience of anger or other strong emotion, the presence of which is only revealed in dreams, by hypnosis, and through some other uncovering procedure such as psychoanalysis. In connection with the second point, one does not claim that conscious or unconscious emotions (worry, hostility, or anxiety) *cause* hyperacidity or ulcer; rather, that such effects in combination with other factors *contribute to* such changes.

A sophisticated and lucid account of these matters is available in George Engel's book, *Psychological Development in Health and Disease*[3] which may be considered recommended reading for all counselors. For reasons which he explains, Engel divides the physical (somatic) consequences of psychological stress into those associated with (1) compensated states, and (2) decompensated states. Included under the former are, notably, conversion reactions and pain. The latter comprise "somatopsychic-psychosomatic" disorders strictly defined.

An important distinction to remember is that conversion reactions are *symbolic* expressions of unconscious conflicts, whereas other psychosomatic phenomena are more properly seen as the somatic components of affects. If blushing, for example, expresses a repressed sexual wish about which one is in conflict, it is a conversion symptom. If, by contrast, blushing simply goes along with being very angry, it is a somatic component of that particular affect. The famous lexicographer, Dr. Samuel Johnson, who was very hypertensive, is supposed to have remarked that his life was in the hands of any scoundrel who chose to make him angry. This makes a somatic component into a racket, if not a conversion symptom!

The range of conversion symptoms is considerable, and counselors—particularly physicians—will encounter many of them. Here is a partial list of conversion reactions:

1. *Affecting motor functions*:
   a. Paralysis or weakness
   b. Seizures: general or local
   c. Other abnormal movements: e.g., tics
   d. Bizarre postures, gaits, muscular stiffness
   e. Disturbances of voice, including mutism
   f. Spasm or paralysis of eye or lid muscles

2. *Affecting sensory functions*:
   a. Pain, including hypersensitivity, in any part of the body
   b. Diminished sensation or total loss
   c. "Functional" blindness; tubular vision
   d. "Functional" deafness
   e. Bizarre sensations of heat and cold

3. *Affecting the cardiovascular system*:
   a. "Heartache"
   b. Heart consciousness
   c. Pulse consciousness

4. *Affecting respiratory functions*:
   a. Sighing; excessive breathing; labored breathing
   b. Yawning
   c. Breath holding
   d. Coughing; certain "coughs"

5. *Affecting the upper gastrointestinal tract*:
   a. Loss of appetite; excessive appetite; chronic overeating
   b. Difficulty swallowing; "lump in throat"
   c. Nausea; vomiting
   d. Constant thirst; excessive water intake
   e. "Air swallowing"; abdominal bloating

6. *Affecting the lower gastrointestinal tract*:
   a. Constipation
   b. Diarrhea
   c. Loss of usual control; incontinence

7. *Affecting the urinary tract*:
   a. Excessive, frequent urination
   b. Urgency; difficulty in urinating
   c. Retention of urine
   d. "Wetting"; incontinence

8. *Affecting the genital apparatus:*
   a. Impotence; frigidity
   b. Pseudopregnancy
   c. Genital anesthesia
   d. Vaginismus; other difficult or painful intercourse

9. *Affecting the skin:*
   a. Blushing; blanching
   b. Spontaneous hemorrhage; stigmata

10. *Affecting consciousness and certain psychic func-
    tions:*
    a. Fainting; "becoming faint"
    b. Forgetting; amnesias
    c. Certain kinds of ignorance or stupidity: "Child
    bride," "injured innocence," "blissful igno-
    rance," and comparable states
    d. Conditions associated with school or vocational
    failures: "fatigue," "lack of will power," "no
    ambition," and comparable syndromes
    e. Fugue states, dissociated states, multiple per-
    sonalities, "sleep attacks" (narcolepsy)

It is evident that conversion reactions can imitate or at
least suggest any number of diseases. Here, especially, all
diagnostic possibilities must be considered. Some counselors may settle too quickly for an "organic" diagnosis;
others, for "hysteria." It may be one, the other, or both in
varying proportions, and it may take the team approach to
come up with the final answers.

These are not easy cases, and some are insoluble. It took
repeated examinations and counseling to unravel this one:

A woman patient sought help because of drug addiction secondary to treatment for brain tumor. The tumor was verified by X ray and by neurological examinations. Repeated studies suggested, however, that the neurological findings did not follow an "organic pattern," and counseling was begun. After no more than twenty sessions, this woman "confessed" a secret of many years, after which she rapidly improved, the addiction stopped, and the "brain tumor" disappeared.

The counselor must remember that emotional conflict can be thoroughly repressed. The client is convinced of the physical validity of his suffering or disability. This is the more so in "compensation cases" where continued sickness is rewarded. In postoperative cases there is no proof; there may be scar tissue causing pain or there may be neurotic exaggeration of residual pain or there may be a conversion reaction—or all three. One is too easily tempted, at times, to diagnose malingering.

There appeared in the press this account of such a perplexing case:

A young woman living in Omaha, Nebraska, was in an automobile accident after which she found herself unable to speak except in whispers. Subsequently, she brought suit against the allegedly responsible person, claiming heavy damages for loss of her voice. She refused to cooperate in extensive physical and psychiatric examinations, maintaining that she refused to be "made a guinea pig." This attitude on her part gave rise to the impression that she might be malingering. The court subsequently awarded her a substantial sum of money, most of it to be paid, however, only if she failed to regain her voice within ten years.

One cannot prejudge such a case. It is quite possible that this person has really "lost her voice." The fact that there are no organic physical findings to explain this fact and that the patient resists examinations do not prove malingering; it is just as possible that unconscious emotional conflicts are at the basis of her symptoms. If such is the case, only a deep and thorough investigation of the patient's emotional life, with the discovery of the dynamic psychological purposes behind the symptom, would lead to an understanding and removal of it. Similar situations exist in a considerable percentage of patients who consult physicians and, probably, in many who are the clients of other counselors.

Another example is taken from the records of a municipal psychiatric clinic:

A thirty-five-year-old woman was admitted to the clinic on the recommendation of a social worker connected with a private family casework agency. The patient complained of insomnia, choking sensations when swallowing food, and feelings of depression and fatigability, making it impossible for her to do her housework or take care of her three minor children. The social worker noted that the patient appeared to derive a certain amount of secondary satisfaction from her illness as she made an effort to let her relatives and acquaintances know how sick she felt.

Conversations with the psychiatrist brought out a good deal of feeling with respect to facts already known to the social worker. The patient had very ambivalent feelings toward her aged father in whose home she lived, and toward her husband who had deserted her some years before. In addition, she had for various reasons identified herself with her mother who had died many years before from a brain tumor; and the patient now feared lest she herself, at about the same age, die from a similar disease.

The psychiatrist helped this patient to give up emotionally the husband who had no intention of returning, and to bring out some of the anger she felt both toward him and toward her aged father, by whom she unconsciously wished to be supported. Her home situation improved with a better attitude toward her father and children (toward whom she was likewise ambivalent), and she found it possible to do more housework and take on part-time outside work as well. With this partial improvement, the patient's physical symptoms largely disappeared so that she ate normally and slept better.

The deepest significance of this client's difficulties was never understood in detail, but enough was known to indicate that her insomnia and choking sensations, while eating, masked psychological conflicts centering around her hostilities toward father, deserting husband, and children. When she could become conscious of these, and accept them, she had less need to be ill. A partial proof of this came later when she fell down and injured her back, but did not attempt (unconsciously) to exploit this as she had her earlier symptoms.

B. *Physical Illness As a Retreat From Reality Difficulties*

Physical symptoms and illnesses may not only mask psychological conflicts but they may also represent an escape from them, a retreat from unpleasant reality situations which appear to the individual as intolerable. Perhaps this is a distinction without a marked difference; so far as the unconscious is concerned the same purpose is achieved since, in both instances, the ego defends itself against anxiety, and certain id tendencies find gratification. Nevertheless, there are differences in the external manifestations of these processes, and it is these which the counselor encounters in the first instance.

The following case illustrates one such situation:

A forty-two-year-old married woman entered a state hospital with a history of having spent the previous fifteen years in her bedroom and the last five of these years in bed. Her husband had spent a small fortune on medical care for her varied, but always elusive, complaints, and both the husband and a twenty-year-old daughter (the only child) had become accustomed to planning their lives so that one of them was always at home with her. The cause of the patient's invalidism remained entirely obscure.

After a few weeks in the hospital, without intensive treatment of any kind, a remarkable change occurred in this patient. Instead of lying constantly in bed, being waited upon hand and foot, she was up and about taking care of many of her own needs. Later she was climbing stairs easily; later still, she willingly helped nurses and attendants with the care of other patients.

From psychological material which later became available, it appeared that to this woman a growing daughter was a threat. She feared unconsciously that her youthful daughter would take her place in her husband's affections; and this threat to her security stirred up strong, but unconscious, hostilities toward both the daughter and the husband. Her illness served two principal purposes: it bound the husband to her, so that he could not get away; and it kept the daughter always in sight, so that she could not take her father away from the patient. In addition, the patient expressed the hostilities she felt toward both of them by compelling them radically to restrict their pleasures and to wait upon her like two slaves. The patient thus retreated from a (to her) intolerable situation and achieved a new type of security on the basis of illness. The final refusal of the husband and daughter to permit such an adjustment, plus the insight the patient obtained in the hospital, broke what had become a vicious cycle, and permitted her to make a more mature type of adjustment.

The same type of situation can arise, of course, under the pressure of external threats to one's security. The loss of a job, desertion by one's wife or husband, failure of a wheat crop, or any comparable source of stress from the environment may arouse sufficient anxiety to produce in certain individuals a similar "retreat into illness."

C. *Psychological Symptoms in Physical Illness*

The psychological symptoms of acute physical illness range from the mild irritability of anyone in discomfort to the hallucinations and irrationality of a psychosis. Some individuals appear to be especially susceptible to the toxins of an illness such as pneumonia, for example, or to the high temperature that may accompany such illnesses:

A twenty-five-year-old medical student, sick with a streptococcus sore throat, had a temperature of 105 degrees Fahrenheit on several successive days. It was observed that every time the fever arose above about 104.6 degrees this patient first became delirious, and then developed auditory hallucinations. He believed he heard his father's voice in the hall outside his hospital room, and he struggled to get out of bed to go to his father. In reality, his father was many miles away, and it took the efforts of several nurses to restrain him in bed. When his temperature fell below 104 degrees this patient was perfectly rational, and had no recollection of his psychotic behavior.

In every illness the forces of repression are weakened to a greater or less extent. Depending upon factors which are difficult to evaluate, anxieties are stirred up and unconscious strivings tend to assert themselves. Various ego defenses are then called into play and appear in various forms: irritability, suspiciousness, regression to childishness, increased demands upon other persons, or even, as in the case cited above, psychotic productions. Thus, the latent (unconscious) wish to be taken care of, as during childhood, may reappear during illness in the form of helplessness, demanding tendencies, and other forms of regressive behavior; or, the ego defenses against these tendencies may be strengthened, so that the patient regards being helpless as a threat, reacting with irritability, resentment against the nurses, and exaggerated independence. Other persons with unconscious self-punitive needs even interfere with treatment measures and prejudice their chances for recovery.

Two unusual reactions to illness were observed simultaneously in one of the wards of a county hospital:

A senior intern taking over a female surgical service from his predecessor was told that two young women were awaiting operations for appendicitis; neither case was acute. The girl in bed No. 1 soon pestered the new intern with demands to be operated upon at once; the girl in bed No. 6 made no such demands, but was calm and content to wait for the next regular operating day. The first girl's eagerness for an operation aroused the intern's suspicions of some neurotic mechanism, but the attending surgeon ordered both cases prepared for surgery the next day.

The next morning found both patients ready for operations; the first girl was almost ecstatic in her white gown, and announced that she was a bride going to her wedding. Despite the intern's heightened qualms, she went to the operating table. Both patients had uneventful, simple appendectomies. Two days after the operations, however, the nurses discovered the girl in bed No. 1 interfering with her surgical dressings, and the next day caught her manipulating the wound itself with her hand. As was almost inevitable, she developed a severe peritonitis and died several days later.

At midnight, following this death, the intern came into the ward only to find that the second girl, who until then had been convalescing normally, had "gone into a trance." The night surgeon and several interns were pinching and in other ways trying to arouse the patient. When these efforts failed, the intern in charge, assuming that the girl was in a self-induced hypnotic sleep, "suggested" to her that she go into a normal sleep and wake up as usual the next morning. This the patient did, with no recollection of her nocturnal trance. The intern then encouraged her to talk to him and discovered that she was greatly worried, first of all, because her mother had not written to her for some days, and secondly, because she assumed that, since she was operated upon at the same time as the girl in bed No. 1, she too might die. This chance to discuss her worries and a little reassurance from the intern were sufficient to relieve the girl's anxiety, and she went on to an uneventful recovery.

It is evident that the intern's initial impression about the first girl was correct. What he lacked was the training and experience to see that a self-destructive psychosis lay close beneath her obviously neurotic wish to have an operation. The second girl's trance was, on the contrary, simply an escape from severe anxiety; a regression to a state of oblivion. Although somewhat exaggerated, these two situations illustrate emotional episodes that often arise in connection with some acute medical or surgical condition.

Chronic illnesses may produce psychological symptoms also, although ordinarily not of such marked severity. Individuals with hitherto latent demanding tendencies or wishes to be cared for on an infantile level may find, in chronic sickness or disability, "excuses" for the expression and gratification of such tendencies. Or, again, the defenses against these wishes may become more predominant. Many persons who, in Adlerian terms, "compensate" for their organic deficiencies are really manifesting strong reaction formations against the wishes which might be expressed through exploitation of illness or disability. They thus go to the opposite extreme of achieving mastery over their limitations and defending themselves against the repressed infantile drives. Often such reaction formations take highly constructive form and make for conspicuous success. It is possible that the accomplishments of Beethoven, despite deafness, Theodore Roosevelt, despite early illness and physical weakness, and others are constructive examples of this defense mechanism.

D. *Clients and Drugs*

Counselors of all professional backgrounds are seeing an increasing number of clients who are taking tranquilizers, energizers, or other medications. A caricature of what one may encounter is seen in the "dexamyl-seconal set" whose members take the former to keep going by day, and the latter to sleep at night. Aldous Huxley is supposed to have suggested that we all need tranquilizers, and it has been asserted that Mahatma Gandhi constantly sipped a tranquilizing tea. When someone asked Huxley, "But what about psychoanalysis?" he is supposed to have answered: "But if you're analyzed, you *really* need the stuff!"

These comments are not an apology or a defense. They simply state a condition. The narcotics problem is a familiar one. A newer and less familiar one arises in connection with the drugs that elevate the mood, calm the nerves, or put us to sleep at night.

Patients undergoing psychoanalysis are urged—if not ordered—to avoid such drugs. The reasons are quite valid. It is important for the success of the analysis that they face their anxieties, their depression, or their insomnia. It is part of the analytic work to understand these symptoms, and this may be difficult or impossible to do if the symptoms are anesthetized by drugs.

There are, however, indications for the use of drugs even in psychoanalysis. The patient works best when there is an *optimum level* of distress, not if he is overwhelmed by it. Panic, for example, disrupts the analytic situation just as any other actual pain may do. The question is that of what impedes or what facilitates the analytic process, not that of absolute rules.

Counselors who have been psychoanalyzed sometimes carry rigid attitudes about drugs into their own professional work. If they are not physicians, they may be afraid to inquire about such matters, and beyond this they may regard drugs as forbidden. It is better to fall back upon general principles than rigid rules: What helps or hinders the counseling?

Counseling interviews at intervals of once a week or less

frequently are not the same as analytic sessions every day. The client's objectives are not the same, his ego functions differently, and the nature of the relationship is different. The counselor working intensively with a client may well advise him to cut down on medications that mask or narcotize his feelings, but this is in a different context and with somewhat different indications than is the case with psychoanalysis.

A consideration of great importance is whether the client's medications are under medical supervision. Self-medication is potentially dangerous, particularly if the client—as happens not uncommonly—is using prescriptions obtained at different times from different doctors. An occasional client will play one prescribing source against another and, in the process, accumulate a considerable supply of medicines. For various reasons, then, the counselor needs to know what medicines the client is taking and whether their use is supervised. At the same time, he can acknowledge that drugs are, at times, like crutches; they can help to support a fractured ego, but hopefully they will be put aside in time.

Another problem about drugs comes from their extensive use in public mental hospitals. Many patients, nowadays, are stabilized quite rapidly with drugs and, once stabilized, are discharged. These patients leave the hospital with detailed instructions about the continued use of the drugs and about adequate follow-up treatment, but many do not follow through. A recent survey of mental hospital readmissions showed that 75 per cent were those who had discontinued the use of the drugs prescribed for them or who were not getting a sufficient dose.

All counselors, including physicians, must appreciate the dramatic changes in mental hospital practice because of the "psychoactive" drugs. As the length of hospital care is shortened, the need for individualized aftercare increases. The discharged patient reenters a family and a community (including the medical community) that is unfamiliar with the drugs and, often, hostile to them. The counselor who gets these former patients as clients may find it necessary to become an expert on the drugs himself, at least to the extent of getting the hospital's recommendations and interpreting them to the patient and his family.

Hostility to the drugs is justified, of course, if treatment stops with them. It is not enough simply to empty out the mental hospitals. Properly used, the drugs make otherwise psychotic patients accessible to psychotherapy and to other forms of treatment, leading to self-integration and reintegration in the community. To put it simply: The drugs increase the need and opportunity for counseling, and they are frequently collaborating, not conflicting, therapies.

Much the same may be said about "shock treatment." Despite the abuse of some forms of shock therapy in the past, and the damage that can be done, it is still the consensus of informed psychiatrists—including leading psychoanalysts—that a limited number of shock treatments given under careful supervision may be the treatment of choice for certain depressive reactions. When thus indicated, shock therapy may shorten the course of a depression and facilitate psychotherapy and other methods of treatment.

1. Morton F. Reiser, "Psychosomatic Illness," *Encyclopedia of Mental Health*. Deutsch, Albert and Fishman, Helen, eds., (New York: Franklin Watts, Inc., 1963), pp. 1710–1721.

2. Bela Mittelmann and Harold G. Wolff, "Emotions and Gastroduodenal Function: Experimental Studies on Patients with Gastritis, Duodenitis and Peptic Ulcer," *Psychosomatic Medicine*, 4:5–61, 1942.

3. George L. Engel, *Psychological Development in Health and Disease* (Philadelphia: W. B. Saunders Company, 1962).

CHAPTER ELEVEN

Footnotes on Treatment

Nearly everything in this book has implications for treatment. Clients come to us with problems. What we provide, broadly speaking, is consultation leading to treatment or treatment itself. Diagnosis indicates the most appropriate treatment. Resistance, regression, and transference are phenomena of the treatment process. The attempt to resolve conflicts and to solve problems may be seen as treatment whatever the intensity, depth, or severity of the conflicts or problems. For present purposes, then, it is treatment whether it is called therapy, psychotherapy, casework, or counseling.

We are about to discuss ways in which treatment can be classified. This will give organization to topics of earlier chapters and of collateral reading. We wish here to take a broad view. We acknowledge at the outset, however, that no system avoids overlapping and no classification is complete. Granting this, we add the following footnotes on counseling classified (1) according to its aims; (2) according to the role of the counselor; (3) according to the principal methods and techniques used by the counselor; and (4) according to the diagnosis of the client's personality in relation to his problems.

A. *Goals and Aims of Counseling*

Writings about the goals and aims of counseling present semantic difficulties. Authors avoid monotonous repetition of the same terms by using words that are synonymous according to some usages, but are distinct according to others. *Goals*, *aims*, and *objectives*, for example, have the same or different connotations in different books or articles.

The *goal* of counseling is obviously to help the client. More formally, it is to improve the individual's total functioning. This might, as well, be called the aim or the objective. Some writers, however, have another use for *aim* as we shall see in the following paragraphs. The analogy is that of war. The goal is to win the war, but the aim or aims are those of strategies, whereas methods and techniques are more akin to tactics and lesser maneuvers. For our purposes, however, general ideas are more important than particular words.

The goal, then, is to help. This may be accomplished in a variety of ways. In order to achieve the goal, according to one classification, the aim may be (1) that of maintaining the client's adaptive patterns; (2) that of modifying adaptive patterns; or (3) that of personality reorganization.[1] These, so to speak, are possible grand strategies.

Others limit themselves to two basic aims. One is essentially to support the client in ways that may maintain or change his habitual adaptive patterns. The other envisions a permanent reorganization in his personality. The broad aims, from this point of view, are thus either supportive or reconstructive in their intent. Each, of course, will have its appropriate methods and techniques.[2]

Florence Hollis, pointing out that supportive treatment does more than maintaining adaptive patterns, defines the treatment aims of counseling as (1) supportive treatment, and (2) the development of self-awareness. She says:

> My definition of the former is "treatment that aims to improve general functioning of the person without substantial increase in the ego's understanding of previously hidden aspects of the self." My definition of the latter is "treatment that holds as a major aim the improvement of the individual's functioning by seeking to better the ego's direction of behavior through enabling the ego to gain more accurate and more complete understanding of previously hidden aspects of the individual's own feelings and behavior." [3]

Other statements of aims are closely tied in with descriptions of the role of the counselor and of methods that he employs. These will be taken up in subsequent sections.

It is important also to distinguish between urgent, intermediate, and long-term aims in treatment. If a client is starving, an urgent aim is that he be fed. The long-term treatment aim will depend upon whether he was starving because he was unemployed, feebleminded, schizophrenic, locked in the attic by cruel parents, or aged, infirm and unable to get to a grocery store. By the same token, a counselor must often support a client during the acute upset of a divorce before suggesting reflective consideration of how it came about.

Hollis points out that other factors determine treatment aims: (1) the motivation of the client, and (2) the etiology of the problems.[4] The original treatment aims of the counselor can be one thing, and what the client agrees to do about them another. Motivation differs with degree of suffering, age, social class, secondary gain, unconscious gratifications, and other variables. Also, motivation can change as when a client, forced to come initially, discovers for himself that he can gain from counseling and thereafter comes willingly.

The factor of causation or etiology is of manifest importance. One has to determine what can and what cannot be changed. Marital conflicts based upon deep-seated neurotic interaction are unlikely to yield to counseling. External limits to the aims of counseling are imposed by conditions over which the counselor has no control: war, death, unemployability, congenital deformity, limited intelligence, and so on. There are times when acceptance of hard facts is the only possible treatment aim. Few choices are so cruel, but limited objectives are at times the only ones realizable.

B. *The General Role of the Counselor*

Classification of treatment according to the predominant role of the counselor suggests the following: (1) counselor-centered counseling, (2) client-centered counseling, and (3) group-centered counseling. Who is at the center of the counseling relationship? Who, to put it boldly, does the talking? This is the essence of such a classification.

Counselor-centered counseling is often not considered treatment. It is perhaps more characteristic of consultation. It is counselor-centered when the counselor gives orders, instruction, findings, information, suggestions, or advice. The unconsciously authoritarian counselor may impose counselor-centered treatment without knowing it. The hallmark, in any case, is the counselor's actual preeminence in the relationship.

Educative and "limit-setting" therapies become counselor-centered by the activity of the counselor. This is the case when the counselor offers himself as an object for a client's new and healthier identifications. This approach can be very useful in the treatment of adolescents or adults unable to tolerate insight therapies. The assumption by a counselor of major activity and responsibility in treatment must, however, be very carefully considered lest it deprive the client of self-determination and self-reliance.

Client-centered counseling puts the client at the center of the treatment. Granting the activity of the counselor in relationship, environmental manipulation and other techniques, it is the client who talks, reacts, gains strength, and makes decisions. His autonomy remains predominant. This is what the term *counseling* usually implies, and it has been the central topic of all preceding chapters.

In nondirective client-centered counseling the counselor is generally the least active of all. Taking for granted the inner resources of the client, the nondirective counselor allows the client's flow of words and feelings and the relationship itself to work their therapeutic effects. The counselor summarizes for the client what the latter has said so that he may hear it in more objective terms. Or, he may point out the essence of the client's revelations, thus indicating central trends or themes. This, of course, is a kind of confrontation and suggests an emphasis, but even so the counselor is *relatively* nondirective.

Group-centered counseling includes group therapy, couples' groups, family counseling, and marital counseling when husband and wife are seen together. Attention is directed to interaction within the group as well as to the individual's reactions to the group. The aim varies in group-centered therapies in that it is sometimes to help the individual through his participation in a group, whereas at other times it is to preserve and strengthen the group itself, as with a marriage or an entire family-treated ensemble. Group treatment may therefore be client-centered, group-centered, or both. It is a matter of common experience, we should add, for persons to begin in group therapy and then change over, at their own request, to individual treatment.

C. *Principal Techniques of Counseling*

In Chapter 1 we classified the techniques of counseling as (1) supportive relationship, (2) environmental manipulation, (3) clarification, and (4) interpretation. Such a classification can be much more elaborate. Methods available to the counselor in relationship therapy include, for example, suggestion, persuasion, reassurance, reasoning, and the giving of advice. Interpretation, again, offers a number of possibilities as to what to interpret and when. Environmental manipulation takes many forms.

Any listing of techniques of counseling has more meaning when subordinated to treatment aims. From this point of view, relationship therapy and environmental manipulation are techniques aimed predominantly at improving a client's functioning without substantial increase in insight, whereas clarification and interpretation are quite definitely aimed at increasing his self-awareness and understanding. A rational treatment plan, taking account of a diagnostic estimation of a client's needs and potentialities, first sets forth the aims and then the techniques calculated to achieve them.

Such planning cannot ignore, however, what the client himself brings to the treatment situation. This is no reason for the counselor to change his strategies, but it is reason for him not to claim too much for them. An advertisement once ran in a New York paper: *"Listening: $5 Per Hour."* Nothing more! And the listener had no dearth of clients. We infer from this that silent attention is sufficient therapy for many troubled people.

The early psychoanalyst, S. Ferenczi, quoted Sigmund Freud as having said that while "we may treat a neurotic in any way we like, he always treats himself psychotherapeutically, that is to say, with transferences." [5] We do not always know, in other words, what emotional strength a client takes from what we say or from our silence, our drugs or our placebos, our environmental manipulation or our interpretations.

The Father of French Surgery, Ambrose Paré, is quoted as saying, "I dressed the wound, and God healed it." The same attitude is appropriate in counseling. The client brings some kind of innate healing potentialities to the relationship, and these are activated whatever the counselor's technical approach may be. Even the quiet listener heals via the client's transferences because he refrains from panic, accusation, retaliation, or condemnation. Listening alone is in contrast to the client's fearful expectations, and this frees him for more dispassionate reflection on his problems. This assumes, however, that the client does not take it as a hostile silence.

There is no reason to regard this as a mystique. The tides of such unconscious interaction are much less obscure to a psychoanalyst because the analysis itself is devoted to rendering them conscious. In other therapies the same unconscious forces play their roles, and they seem mysterious only in remaining unconscious. The emotional *vis medicatrix naturae*—the healing power of nature—is no more obscure than that of other healing processes once we have the proper instruments for observation.

This, then, is but a footnote to earlier paragraphs (Chapter 5) on the power of relationship. It is not merely that the counselor, because of the client's transferences, is endowed with godlike powers for good or ill. It is also that the client, silently utilizing such transference images, can cure himself in the relationship by what he takes from it in the way of hope, permission, forgiveness, acceptance, greater objectivity about himself, and other attitudes that make for strength and greater self-determination.

D. *Techniques According to Diagnosis*

The clinical vignettes of previous chapters make it clear that diagnosis is not a simple matter. If rational treatment must be geared to diagnosis, as we have asserted, it is a diagnosis of the total personality of the client and of the total environment in which his adaptive activities are somehow ineffectual. This, as we have seen, involves careful evaluation of such elements as environmental pressures, stress reactions, ego strengths and weaknesses, and the extent to which internal or external components of the total situation can be favorably modified.

Granting that it is essential to individualize, we nevertheless use diagnostic labels. They provide us with generalizations that have the validity of rules of thumb. Their value is in giving us an initial orientation to treatment. They cease to have value in a specific situation, however, unless the counselor has the ability to change as the client, the external situation, or the total interaction changes. With all due caution, then, we offer certain generalizations about treatment classified by diagnosis.

It is a rule of thumb in psychoanalysis that a patient must have better than average intelligence and, beyond that, to have what is vaguely termed "psychological-mindedness." This implies that he must have some capacity for self-examination, for tolerating free association, and for accepting the illogic of his subjective life. He must be able to form a relationship, acknowledge transference, and develop an observing ego that can stand apart in collaboration with the analyst during a long, tedious, and sometimes frightening examination of his hitherto unconscious self.

These considerations hold to some extent for any insight therapy. Clarification and interpretation are of little use if the client is unable to grasp their intent and use whatever they reveal. Such techniques are fruitless for clients for whom some clinical diagnoses are apt.

Clients of limited intelligence, education, or cultural advantages are likely to need and do better with environmental manipulation, supportive relationship, and educational measures than with clarification or interpretation. They will use only what they can comprehend in concrete terms. They are likely to run away from what baffles and therefore frightens them. Emotional security in relationship may, of course, reveal previously hidden capacities. If this occurs it changes the diagnosis and, accordingly, the treatment plan.

Adolescents, schizophrenics, and clients with acting-out personality disorders usually tolerate clarification poorly and interpretation not at all. Insight requires an ability to cope with anxiety, and for such clients increased anxiety becomes intolerable. They may panic, run from treatment, act out more seriously than before, or even develop symptoms of psychosis. Others, by contrast, accept interpretations eagerly, talk about them constantly, and incorporate them into intellectualizing defenses. The counselor's words are used for narcissistic gratification, in other words, but not for therapeutic gain. For such clients supportive relationship, discussion of current reality problems, and whatever environmental changes may be indicated are much better therapy than is insight.

Clients who have been released from psychiatric hospitals or discharged from other psychiatric treatment frequently have similar needs. Their psychic wounds are healing over and should not be further opened up. Clients who have been refused service by psychiatric clinics are poor risks for insight therapies if refusal was on the basis of careful evaluation. Clients whose ego strengths must be sustained by medications are poor risks for other than supportive and environmental measures.

Some clients' defenses are such that self-examination is made impossible by projection. This is true of those correctly labeled paranoid. They have no conscious anxiety or guilt and therefore no available incentive to use clarification or interpretation. In their eyes it is the environment that should be treated: a wife, a boss, the size of the relief check, the top brass of the Army, and so on. They can often be helped by firm confrontation with the realities of life and of their particular circumstances. Careful and patient counseling along these lines may pave the way to introspective reflection, but initial techniques should usually focus on externals.

Whatever the diagnosis, counseling must always respect a client's defenses. They protect the client against anxiety, regression and, at times, disintegration. To bypass or strip away defenses is to invite serious trouble. Interpretations out of the context of therapy (as in "parlor analysis") are rightly taken as an attack, and premature interpretation in treatment, if not simply warded off, has the same impact. The client needs his defenses or he would not have them, and he will give them up when he feels secure enough to do so. Once a good relationship has been established, however, it is a mistake not to deal with matters that a client is clearly hinting at. Failure to do so increases the client's anxiety and sometimes leads to acting out.

In predominantly reactive or situational conditions, environmental change is usually the all-important treatment aim. The client requires a chance to reassert his usual ego functioning more than to examine it. Relieve the pressures, he might say, and he can once more manage very well. He may gain self-understanding in the process, inasmuch as changes do not occur in a vacuum, but the primary techniques are other than, say, interpretation.

E. *Further Reflections on Treatment*

Writings on counseling as therapy are bound to be somewhat vague at times. One reason is that training for and experience in treatment are so uneven among the several professional groups concerned. It does not help, of course, that vocabularies are frequently so different. Another reason is that so much remains to be learned about what works and what does not work even for the supposedly most sophisticated therapists. There are those who assert that psychoanalysis is the only definitive treatment method for problems of personal adjustment, while others prefer to remain eclectic and state that each therapist, like each artist, must develop his own techniques. It is safer to assert, perhaps, that there are effective and less effective methods and techniques, depending upon a client's needs as well as the counselor's skills, and that each therapist develops his own *style* in using them. In any case, it is all too easy to bog down in rival claims obscured by difficult semantics.

The fact remains, however, that there are gross differences in therapeutic sophistication. As these pages are being written, the morning paper reports a striking medical discovery. Sexual frigidity can be cured, the announcement states, by the use of hypnosis to uncover the one traumatic sexual experience in a woman's life that has produced her unhappy symptom. Freud and Breuer knew this, of course, by 1892. There is an extensive literature since that time on the limitations both of the notion of any one traumatic experience as the cause and of hypnosis as a cure. Some laymen could have set the reporting doctor straight, not to mention most social workers, many psychologists, and numerous clergymen.

But there is more to vagueness and confusion than honest ignorance. It stems also from limitations of our training and things as yet undiscovered about the therapeutic process itself. How the client uses relationship, for example, is frequently unknown to us. It is impossible to distinguish its effect from the impact of our own endeavors. The same interpretation can be made innumerable times, for example, but why it "clicks" now when it never has before is something that frequently eludes us. The therapeutic importance of external happenings in the course of treatment is sometimes crystal clear, but it may be totally obscure whether this has been pure accident or unconscious design so far as the activity of the client is concerned.

A valid claim of psychoanalysis is this: The more one has the chance to witness the operation of unconscious processes, the less mysterious are the processes of therapy. The psychoanalyst does not see everything, but he has the opportunity to see more than most. Even so, as we have stated, much remains unknown to him. As counselors, we offer to the client a treatment program that we think is indicated and that we hope will be effective, but when it works we are not always certain how or why. As therapists, therefore, all of us stand somewhere between the innocence of Lady Bountiful and the hoped-for wisdom of the years that lie ahead.

F. *Termination of Treatment*

There are two important aspects of bringing counseling to an end. One is *when* to do it, and the other is *how*. Some situations present no problems but others are far from simple. We shall discuss here some aspects of termination where counseling has gone beyond the phase of consultation and has involved more than a casual interpersonal relationship.

The obvious time to terminate is when the client has solved his presenting problems. Suppose that Mrs. Smith came in a panic about a recommended surgical operation. She has largely mastered her anxieties and is prepared to go ahead with surgery. Counseling can stop with the understanding that she is free to return if other difficulties arise. Or, Mr. Jones was undecided about divorce, but has come to a decision. He and Mrs. Jones have agreed to put the matter "on the shelf" while both undergo psychoanalysis. Counseling stops as another treatment plan begins.

These, however, are not the difficult decisions. What if the client feels better, has made decisions and is satisfied with his solutions, but the counselor sees other and more pervasive difficulties? The client's wish to terminate at this point may represent a fear of transference feelings, defense against dependency, flight into health, or some other form of resistance. The counselor must confront the client with such possibilities, but should not press the point too far. The counselor is obligated to respect defenses of the client that the latter cannot relinquish easily. Unless the counselor is prepared to psychoanalyze, he must often settle for a symptomatic cure; i.e., reduction of the client's anxiety and guilt, and overall improvement in the client's functioning.

The counselor's decision depends partly on the original treatment contract. Just what was the agreement to work together? Did the counselor suggest limited treatment aims or make it clear that insight therapy would be involved? In any case the client is entitled to his defenses unless modification of his personality has been agreed upon as a treatment plan and the counselor is fully prepared to work with whatever lies behind the defensive structures and operations of the client.

The counselor is frequently the last to know that a client is ready for termination. Clients have a way of improving in their external lives while apparently having greater difficulties in the therapy. Unless the counselor listens "in between the lines" he may miss the extent of the client's improvement. In other words, the client is repeating his emotional problems with the counselor more than with others in the external environment. Transference reactions have intensified in the treatment and the counselor must help the client to understand and otherwise resolve them.

Apart from this, the client often wishes to prolong the treatment despite improvement. Its gratifications are considerable and he is naturally reluctant to give them up. In order to continue, he will try to please the counselor by bringing in more and more to talk about. Somehow there is a new crisis every week. Or, as the client goes on with interviews, he manages to avoid applying insights to his outside reality problems. He learns more to please the counselor than to change himself. Emotional forces within the client often favor interminable counseling, and the counselor is frequently hard put to it to cope with these and bring the relationship to an end.

Criteria for termination revolve about two principal areas of the counseling. One is that of the client's presenting problems and the other that of his relationship to the counselor. So far as the former are concerned, termination is indicated when the problems have been solved, when a way to their solution has been delineated, when—even though they are not solved—the client is strong enough to find his own solutions, or when it becomes clear that nothing further can be accomplished by means of counseling. Client and counselor alike must sometimes agree to settle for limited goals or even agree that further work together is profit-less. Occasionally this becomes a painful unilateral decision, but it can be foolish and destructive not to make it.

The crucial factors are the client's ego strengths and the environment with which the client must contend. If the former have reached an optimal potential and the latter is as favorable as the realities of life permit, then termination is clearly indicated. We can generally assume that thera-peutic gains continue after the counseling has ended, because full consolidation of ego strengths occurs with emancipa-tion from the counseling relationship itself.

This is an aspect of the second area of counseling; i.e., that of the relationship to the counselor. We have seen already that resistance, regression, and transference phe-nomena are inevitable components of the relationship. Re-gression as a stress reaction is replaced by regression in the counseling relationship itself. Intensification of transferences is a by-product of this regression. Much of this will be re-solved during the counseling itself, but some will be laid to rest only after the interviews have stopped. Termination is in order, so far as the relationship itself is concerned, when the client can accept the realities of the relationship and the inevitable limitations of the counseling process. Termina-tion is indicated, also, if the client cannot accept such limi-tations and if it appears that he will never be able to do so. In any case, termination cannot wait for the millennium.

Termination can also be dictated by agency policy or by the time or other limitations of the individual counselor. Counselors are often very reluctant to say, "I cannot help this client further." By the same token, consultants find it equally difficult to state, "This client is untreatable, and you had better terminate." Neither one can read the crys-tal ball and neither can know for certain what might be just around the corner. One must attempt to assert realistic criteria and probabilities and to put aside deep wishes for omnipotence or irrational needs to cure.

The following vignettes highlight the problems. The answers will vary with individual agencies and counselors:

1. The widow mentioned earlier spoke in the initial interview of conflicts about expelling an unwelcome boarder and selling her unwieldy home. Two years later neither problem had been resolved. Actually, they were connected. With the boarder's help, the big house was manageable; without him it was not. The consultant felt that the woman's neurotic tie to the boarder went too deep for counseling. He could only recommend that this aspect of the problem be dropped and the client be encouraged to get into activities that would maintain lifelong compulsive defenses. This done, he felt, the counseling could terminate.

2. A woman of about thirty began psychoanalysis because her marital problems appeared to be symptomatic of neurosis. Her husband refused treatment. In the analysis some premature confrontations or interpretations sent her into panic and severe regression. The patient ran from her analyst only to become involved with a succession of other therapists. Her unconscious masochism led her into situations in which she was very badly treated. She was somewhat stabilized by drugs, but refused to take them consistently. The recommendation was finally made that all interpretive and "analyzing" efforts stop. The use of supportive relationship and discussion of surface problems was calculated to allow

a healing over of "deeper matters," in which she was floundering as if in quicksand, and to regain some of her defenses albeit without resolution of many conflicts.

3. A married woman of forty sought help intermittently for difficulties involving her mother, a sister, and finally an adopted son. On each occasion she revealed a tendency to manage others and to interfere with the responsibilities of others. Along with this were poorly concealed hostilities and deep strivings to be taken care of herself. Five members of the family were ultimately involved in counseling, but only two appeared to use it constructively. The consultant suggested that the client's personality difficulties were too severe and too strongly defended for counseling, and that the efforts of the agency could most profitably be concentrated on the husband and one daughter.

4. A young married man discussed his problems as a husband and a father. Feelings of inferiority and inadequacy in the marriage predominated. It took some time for the counselor to realize that there were many muted, offhand references to considerable social and business successes. It then appeared that much of the self-depreciation expressed a transference need to appear noncompetitive and ineffectual. At the same time, his self-accusations were a defense against unspoken hostile criticisms of his wife. When these matters could be clarified, it was possible to terminate the counseling on the assumption that the client and his wife must deal with the realities of their relationship.

Termination problems are frequently problems of diagnosis or of countertransference, or both. Counselors are loath to find a client too difficult to treat and, once started, are very reluctant to give up. Long-term cases should be subject to periodic review both of diagnosis and progress in therapy. A reevaluation after every twelve to fifteen interviews is not too frequent!

The *how* of terminating varies, of course, with the extent and intensity of the counseling relationship. An initial interview can end with an agreement about referral or with the counselor's statement that he is unable to provide the service wanted or required. Much the same is an early understanding that counseling will be limited to a consultation or diagnostic function.

Another built-in type of termination exists where limited service has been offered and accepted. This occurs, for example, when there is an understanding at the outset to see how much can be accomplished before the client goes away to college, gets married, or takes another job. Similar to this is counseling limited by the counselor, often because of uncertainties of diagnosis and prognosis, to six or ten or twenty interviews.

A client sometimes panics as the end of interviews approaches, but the counselor should generally be firm about the plan to stop. Having reacted with distress over impending termination, the client can usually tolerate an agreement to try it on his own for six months or so. An actual collapse requires some other kind of treatment in most cases, whereas the trial separation, even with indications of distress, generally paves the way to actual termination.

When counseling has continued to the point where the counselor sees indications for termination, he usually sends up a trial balloon. This takes the form of a passing remark to the effect that the client has now considered his problems pretty thoroughly; or that he appears to be doing most of the problem-solving work himself; or that he is now able to manage his life without outside help; or, finally, that all possible choices open to him have been considered thoroughly. The technical maneuver is that of broaching the subject for the client to react to and discuss in subsequent interviews.

Resistive and regressive phenomena may be expected. More important criteria are whether any really new material emerges and whether the client can accept explanations of his unrealistic wishes to continue. He may repeat all of the turmoil that has gone before, but usually in briefer, less disruptive fashion. Generally this is counterbalanced by plans, or hints of plans, for new activities after the counseling is over. When this sort of thing continues over the period of a few interviews, the counselor can return to the subject of termination, setting a date himself or suggesting that the client do so.

It is better for the client to set the date. It is, for him, an exercise in "active mastery." Too much of life is suffered passively. Throughout life, including counseling itself, important relationships are, or often appear to be, at the mercy of others. A person feels stronger and more accepting of reality if he is in a position to say, "I know that I won't like this but I propose to do it anyway."

The counselor must take the initiative, of course, when he decides that further counseling will be to no avail. If he has exhausted his resources, if the client cannot accept the actual limitations of the relationship or other resources of counseling, or if, for whatever reason, the process promises to be unending, it is up to the counselor to call a halt. This requires both tact and firmness. The words will vary with the occasion, but the essential message will be, "We have done all that we can together and we had better make plans to stop." This leaves time for discussion and working through, but it sets the stage for early termination.

The counselor should not blame himself or reject the client. He announces his decision on the basis of realistic considerations. The limitations may be his own or those of the agency or other setting in which he works. They may, on the other hand, be rooted in the client's pathology or in the harsh realities of environmental circumstance. "Some things in you," he may have to say, "are beyond my ability to help." Or, "Some things in life cannot be changed by either of us." There may be other solutions, but not within the province of counseling.

The final interview is generally like any other one. The client may recapitulate or summarize, but there is seldom reason for the counselor to do so. Whatever the turmoil of recent days or weeks, the client frequently astonishes the counselor by indications of composure and maturity. He may go out in tears but surprisingly often will flash a smile and thank the counselor for the benefits he feels. There is seldom reason for the counselor not to smile, shake hands, and wish the client luck or *bon voyage*.

Some clients will ask the counselor to repeat things that he has said or to give detailed suggestions and instructions. If the client does not already know these things, he is unlikely to absorb them now. The counselor can usually remind the client, "You summarized these things yourself not long ago, remember?" Or he can assure him, "What we have discussed will come back to you when you need it." The client's request is sometimes really a testing of the counselor, as if to say, "Have you *really* passed the torch of self-sufficiency to me?"

With termination the counselor must firmly refuse all invitations for a social or other personal relationship. Just as the client must give him up, so he must be able to let the client go. Flat refusal, however, is tactless and unrealistic. Circumstances of life and mutual interests may make ultimate friendship inevitable and desirable. The counselor at the time of termination cannot, nevertheless, encourage such relationships or promise them. He can point out that it takes time for aspects of the professional relationship to wear off and for the client to reestablish his autonomy. Neither can predict what the future may hold, but for now the relationship must be suspended. The counselor, if he needs reminding, should recall the situation of the little boy who proposes to marry Mamma when he grows up. It is not too long before someone else is incomparably more attractive!

Questions of telephone calls, correspondence, or follow-up visits should be answered according to the individual client and his total situation. A wait-and-see attitude is often indicated. One seldom shuts the door irrevocably against further counseling. One strives to put the client on his own and to strengthen his autonomy without depriving him of badly needed help at times of crisis or relapse.

Some clients need to come back once. It is as if they wish unconsciously to check the resolution of their transferences. Some return more than once, but still use the interviews constructively to reinforce what has previously been largely but not entirely understood and resolved. Still others will drop in or telephone on very infrequent occasions as if expressing a need to maintain even the most tenuous of relationships. They are carried along, it seems, simply by the knowledge that the counselor (or the agency) is still there.

It would be unrealistic not to mention those situations in which treatment simply peters out. Counseling may terminate when the client moves away or gets another job or for some reason "just can't make it." Sometimes the relationship ends in mutual frustration, and the client just stops coming. There may be fewer planned than unplanned terminations.

When these occur it is in order for the counselor to review the course of treatment and to figure out, if he can, what contributed to this kind of outcome. Such review is a useful exercise in studying the vicissitudes of counseling relationships. Consultation may reveal countertransference problems in the counselor and point the way to his preventing them or to seeking therapy for himself.

It is a mistake, however, for the counselor to take himself too severely to task for such apparent failures, unless they are routine. He may be astonished, if he stops to consider the matter, at how frequently he learns, through some grapevine or other, how well some of these clients are doing, how much they appreciate the gains they made, and how often they refer others to the same counselor or agency for help. For every former client that one hears about, there are probably several more who have benefited more than seemed possible at the time of unofficial termination. To refer to Freud again, ". . . he always treats himself psychotherapeutically, that is to say, with transferences."

G. *Rules of Thumb*

1. From the point of view of the *presenting problems*, any one or combination of the following may be sufficient reason to consider termination:

   a. the basic difficulties have been defined and
      1) the client can handle the situation by himself, or
      2) appropriate referral has been agreed upon
   b. the client has made a decision among various possibilities and can proceed alone

c. conflicts discussed initially have been resolved to the satisfaction of the client

d. previously crumbling personality defenses have been reinstated and reinforced to the point that the client can be self-sufficient

e. important behavior patterns have been clarified with resulting improvement in the client's interpersonal relationships

f. crucial insights have been achieved and put to work at the service of the client's total functioning

g. necessary environmental changes have been effected, permitting the client to function effectively

h. a decision has been reached that nothing further can be accomplished at this time and in this setting

2. From the point of view of the *relationship* between client and counselor, any one or combination of the following is sufficient reason to consider termination:

a. the client wants to stop for reasons that may or may not be clear and when resistances, if significant elements in the situation, cannot easily be resolved

b. manifest transferences have been understood and mostly worked through

c. the client sees and accepts the realistic limitations of counselor and counseling

d. there is a flight into health or transference cure that the counselor is not trained to challenge therapeutically

e. there is too much secondary gain for the client and he keeps coming for gratification rather than for further change

f. the counselor's countertransference is such that he cannot control it and it interferes significantly with treatment

g. the counselor, being realistic, must say, "we have accomplished all that we can accomplish under present circumstances."

3. About the treatment process in general:

a. always move at the client's rate of understanding and in accordance with his capacities for change

b. do not get lost in trying to understand everything, but rather focus on essential problems about which something can and should be done

c. if the counselor fails to come to grips with sensitive material, the client may assume that it is too terrible or too frightening for the counselor to talk about and will become more apprehensive himself

d. counseling that promises to change one member of a family without corresponding change in others threatens a dynamic balance between or among them and stirs up resistances that can disrupt the treatment

e. clients have little capacity for introspection or the use of interpretations when their external lives are affected by actual deprivation, sickness, or turmoil for any reason, and therefore supportive measures and environmental change are usually indicated

f. never treat a child or adolescent as an independent individual unless he actually is so, legally and financially

g. the time and expense of careful diagnosis and early consultation with others can often save the considerably greater expense of endless counseling

1. *Scope and Methods of the Family Service Agency*. Report of the Committee on Methods and Scope, Family Service Association of America (New York: Family Service Association of America, 1953), pp. 18–20.

2. *Six Approaches to Psychotherapy*. McCary, James L., ed., (New York: The Dryden Press, 1955), pp. 2–3.

3. Florence Hollis, "Personality Diagnosis in Casework," in *Ego Psychology and Dynamic Casework*, Parad, Howard J., ed., (New York: Family Service Association of America, 1958), p. 84.

4. Florence Hollis, *Casework: A Psychosocial Therapy* (New York: Random House, 1964), pp. 206–211.

5. S. Ferenczi, *Sex in Psychoanalysis* (Boston: Gorham Press, 1916), p. 55.

CHAPTER TWELVE

Some Other Aspects of Counseling

A. *Questions of Focus*

Our discussion of counseling in different settings (Chapter 1) highlighted the diverse professional training and experience of those of us who do counseling. It also brought out the fact—sometimes forgotten—that the nature of counseling may be determined, particularly in its beginning phases, by the client's choice of counselor and the reasons (including unconscious ones) for his choice. Implicit in the data of Chapter 1 are other considerations that we must not ignore. We shall deal with some of them in the present chapter.

One of these is the question of focus. In absolute terms, the question is: Do we concentrate on the *problem* which the client brings to us, or do we concentrate on the *client* with the problem? It is possible, of course, to do one or the other; or, it is possible to begin with one and shift to the other. The choice is seldom so black or white, as we have seen; generally it is a matter of emphasis determined both by the client's needs and the function of the counseling service.

It is obvious that counseling may be limited to guidance. What vocation to choose? Where to go to college? What kind of investment to make? What to put into a will? Whether to have a surgical operation? Counseling is involved in all such situations, but it is a kind of counseling that is addressed for the most part to particular problems and to particular needs for guidance. The advice or guidance will, of course, be tailored to the individual. It will take into account his age, talents, health, needs for the future, and so on. From this point of view, the *problem* cannot be isolated from the *person*. At the same time, however, the solution of the problem—in the guidance type of counseling—does not generally require intensive involvement of the total personality makeup of the client in the counseling process.

The situation is quite otherwise when we come to marital counseling, family counseling, child guidance, and the treatment of more extensive psychosocial pathology. The counselor here must be prepared to shift his attention from problems or specific services to the persons who are in need of help. In general, solutions will take longer and the counseling relationships will be more intense and meaningful. The emotional as well as the intellectual lives of both counselor and client will be more deeply involved. Feelings and behavior patterns of which the client was previously unaware play a larger role in these situations; and, to a much greater degree than in finding solutions for particular problems, what we know as personality change may be involved.

Let us not, however, distinguish too sharply between an emphasis upon problems as opposed to persons. Such distinctions are artificial and misleading. An attorney can hardly concentrate upon drawing a will if his client is clearly confused. By the same token, a family counselor must shift his focus if his client is suddenly laid off or has a "coronary." Just as no problem can be dealt with apart from the individual who presents it, so no person can be helped as a person in a vacuum. It is really a matter of emphasis, and even that may shift from day to day or week to week in the person's life experiences and in the counseling relationship.

Questions of focus are not determined exclusively by the client and his difficulties. Most counselors themselves are limited in what they can apprehend. Because of restrictions of training, specialization, "agency function," or similar considerations, few counselors can meet all of the needs of their clients. The guidance counselor, for example, may be required to limit his activities to matters affecting a child's school adjustment, and this may seem impossible when the child's entire family needs intensive casework, if not psychiatric help. The marriage counselor may have been trained in such a way that he is helpless in the face of deeply neurotic interactions between his clients. A physician may lack the time and the training for working with a "school dropout," and yet he is the very person to determine whether defective hearing, poor vision, or some other physical problem is an important factor. Indeed, if he has been a family doctor, he should be the best person to evaluate significant emotional determinants in the maladjustment at school. The psychoanalyst, by virtue of the techniques of his specialty, cannot be a family counselor; and a family counselor, unless he is a physician, cannot prescribe tranquilizers for agitation, or sedatives for insomnia. To some extent, therefore, we are compelled to focus, and none of us is in a position to provide "total care." We must do what, from the client's point of view, we should not have to do!

B. *Aspects of Training*

It would be convenient if we could take for granted the theoretical training of counselors and devote ourselves entirely to a consideration of practical matters. By theoretical is meant, here, everything that contributes to our knowledge of human behavior, of what "makes people tick." The application of such knowledge to particular persons and their individual problems in a counseling relationship constitutes the practice, and therefore the practical aspect, of counseling.

It is a stubborn, practical fact of life, however, that we cannot take our theoretical training for granted. Really satisfactory preparation for counseling would include adequate grounding in all of the behavioral sciences, but few—if any—counselors have such a background. Nearly everyone pays lip service to the ideal of understanding the whole person in the context of his total environment, but almost no one knows enough for such understanding. It is important to stress this point, not because we should forthwith give up our efforts to help others but rather because we should examine our position about professional training in all our disciplines and about collaborative efforts in professional practice.

There is no agreement as to what to include among the behavioral sciences. Nearly every field of learning has something to contribute to a complete science of human behavior. A minimum list would include those sciences that teach us about what we arbitrarily call the physical, the mental, and the environmental determinants of behavior; i.e., for example, anatomy, physiology, psychology, and sociology. In order to understand people's problems, however, we should have to add the study of pathology—organic, psychic, and sociologic. With all of this, however, our knowledge of man is meager unless we add literature, history, comparative religion, philosophy, and perhaps a dozen other fields. The more we know, the better we can understand and, more importantly, the better we can register the sometimes subtle communications that our clients dare not transmit directly.

If we could assume that all counselors were well grounded in the humanities, in man's intellectual and cultural heritage, their training would still be deficient. The physician, for example, is thoroughly trained in "organic medicine" but much less so in psychology and sociology. His medical school exposure to the emotional aspects of illness, to psychiatric illnesses, and to interviewing is seldom followed up in later training or busy private practice. Granting great improvement in recent years, most physicians are not well trained for more than superficial counseling and are not comfortable doing it.

The psychiatrist is better trained, but is often correctly accused of preoccupation with pathology. He is more alert to ego weaknesses than to ego strengths. He may know more about reactions to intrapsychic conflicts than to external stress. He is generally better prepared to understand the individual than the couple or the family as a group. The psychoanalyst, more highly specialized, deliberately restricts himself to the individual and to seeing the world through the eyes of the particular patient.

The social worker based his training originally upon social pathology but, in recent years, has added psychopathology. He knows how to make a psychosocial diagnosis, taking into account genetic, developmental, and longitudinal factors as well as current situational and horizontal determinants. He learns much about personal interactions in marriage and in larger family groups, and about how these carry over into counseling relationships. The conspicuous lack in his training is that of certain aspects of medical training; that is, pathology, psychopathology, and the wider basis for evaluation of symptoms provided by such broader training.

Others who do counseling have equally important limitations. There is no need to labor the point. At the moment, however, we tend to ignore or to minimize the training we ourselves do not have. It would be better, perhaps, to work toward the goal of providing everyone who wants to work therapeutically with human behavior with the widest possible opportunity for understanding human behavior.

It can be argued, however, that these deficiencies of training affect diagnosis more than treatment. It is probably true that experienced counselors of whatever professional background work very much the same way and have comparable skills. The limitations as to diagnostic ability are handled in two ways: one is to discount the importance of diagnosis and even to regard it as a liability; and another is to acknowledge the limitations of the several professions, and to call for a multidisciplinary or "team approach." So far as consideration of theoretical matters is concerned, the breaking down of interdepartmental and interprofessional barriers has become commonplace in universities, special conferences, and centers for advanced study and research. Such collaboration is well established at the clinical level, also, in mental health clinics and psychiatric hospitals where psychiatrists, psychologists, social workers, and other specialists make more unique contributions to diagnosis, perhaps, than to treatment. In matters of differential diagnosis, each has a distinctive contribution to make; as psychotherapists they are increasingly less distinguishable.

The more one realizes that the total personality is involved in even the simple decisions and "problems" of life, the more one is compelled to accept a "diagnostic orientation" in counseling. This does not imply any rigid attitude of "diagnosis must come first" or isolation of "diagnosis" from "treatment." Every counselor would do well to read the first chapter of Erik Erikson's book, *Childhood and Society*, on the first day of each year.

Dr. Brian Bird has recently published a fascinating clinical study that has implications for "normal counseling" of "normal people." He tells of a young mother seeking advice from her physician about some problems with her first child. She asked many questions and seemed sincerely grateful for the advice and suggestions given her. Paradoxically, however, she "forgot" the advice and followed none of the suggestions. What finally became clear, after weeks of perplexity, was that this mother resented the doctor's "child-centered" approach. The mother had her own surgical problem, and the doctor ignored this in regarding the infant as his patient. The mother was jealous of her infant child and angry at the doctor who "neglected" her, and she expressed these feelings by, in effect, destroying his professional effectiveness and punishing the child. This "diagnosis," which led directly to a different focus in counseling, was the result of a multidisciplinary team effort.

C. *Counseling and Psychotherapy*

One might write a book on the differences between counseling and psychotherapy. It would be simpler, however, to assert that they cannot be distinguished. It is all a matter of definitions. It will be enough here to indicate some of the reasons why the distinction has been attempted and to what extent it has validity. One could argue, however, that any kind of professional help is "therapeutic" and that whenever the means of help are predominantly psychological it becomes psychotherapy. It *can* be just as simple as that!

One device for limiting the concept of counseling is to apply the term to situations in which a professional person gives advice or guidance about a particular type of problem or within a circumscribed area of life. The psychological tool employed is principally intellectual. An example is vocational guidance. The counselor gets the facts of the client's interests, aptitudes, and educational level, and he imparts facts, alternatives, and advice tailored to the client's situation. It is clear, however, that such a restricted focus becomes untenable the moment the counselor discovers that the client's hopes are unrealistic or that other problems are relevant to vocational planning.

James F. Adams has attempted the distinction, utilizing the criteria of "depth of the problem" and "intensity of the counseling relationship." [1] There is no absolute distinction but rather a continuum. At one end, the problems are at the surface of conscious awareness, are largely cognitive in nature with little affective involvement, and the counseling relationship is not intense. Toward the other end of the continuum, the relationship, if it is to help, becomes more intense, the problems dealt with are more personal and deepseated, and unconscious factors may have to be taken into account. Adams states that the whole continuum may be considered counseling, but that at some point it merges into and becomes synonymous with psychotherapy.

This, in effect, is the position of many clinical psychologists and social workers. There is a tendency, for example, to give up the term "caseworker" in favor of "counselor," and to accept "intensive casework" or "intensive counseling" as largely synonymous with psychotherapy. Those who would maintain the distinction, however, separate the effects of the counselor-client *relationship* from whatever additional beneficial results may be achieved by *environmental manipulation* such, for example, as financial assistance, foster home placement, provision of new group experiences, and so on. Dr. Maurice Levine and many others, however, would point out that whatever a therapist does has its psychotherapeutic implications, even such medical procedures as making a physical examination or writing a prescription. So, it is clear, in any case, that, depending upon one's predilections, everything can be defined as counseling or as psychotherapy!

The practical aspect of this is that the term counseling is, in fact, being extended to all-inclusive connotations. It cannot be limited any longer to "advice-giving" or guidance. Psychologists, social workers, clergymen, and others employ the term, and when they do they mean to include the processes and the relationships involved in working with people who may have very deep and complicated emotional problems. One among many examples of this trend is to be found in an article by Dr. Frederick Thorne, who is both a psychologist and a psychiatrist. His article, "Directive and Eclectic Personality Counseling," appears in a book entitled *Six Approaches to Psychotherapy*.[2] This book is an excellent illustration of how difficult it is to draw sharp distinctions between counseling and psychotherapy.

In the last analysis, such distinctions are less important than the question as to whether what we are doing is appropriate or not, or is helpful or not. Dr. Maurice Levine has already been mentioned. His book, *Psychotherapy in Medical Practice*,[3] makes it abundantly clear that everything that a doctor does or fails to do has its emotional repercussions and may therefore be psychotherapeutic or not. A somewhat unusual instance of combined counseling-psychotherapy, if you will, in a medical setting occurred when a patient came in from a distant city. She expected to be in the area only a couple of months and she wished to carry on the treatment program already outlined by her psychiatrist at home. The second psychiatrist had little confidence in the treatment already prescribed, but he recognized that this patient's relationship with her doctor was of primary importance. He refrained from disturbing the medicinal regimen in order to preserve intact the larger treatment program; i.e., the continuing relationship with the original psychiatrist.

D. *The Art and Science of Counseling*

The question of appropriateness, implicit in the example just given, suggests a distinction between the science of counseling, and the art. We may consider as the *science* of counseling everything that contributes to a systematic and predictable knowledge of human behavior. The *art*, by contrast, encompasses the often intuitive knowledge of the exceptions and the unpredictable as well as the tact and sense of appropriateness in applying what we know.

There is nothing Delphian about this! Much that seems to be intuitive has been formally learned, and repressed. Much more, perhaps, has been learned unconsciously and informally. Tact is not innate; some of it is developed by early identifications, some by professional supervision and experience. In general, however, the science lies in the formal training and the art is in its application with a given client at a given moment.

The basic sciences, as we have noted, are the behavioral sciences. From these sciences we know, for example, that marriage between a Negro and a white person has two strikes against it. Morally this should not be so, but scientifically it is so. It is *not* a fact that such marriages cannot work; it *is* a fact—statistically speaking—that the majority will be extremely difficult and many will be strained to the breaking point.

What are the relevant scientific facts? One, coming from sociology, is that marriages based upon a similiarity of backgrounds—social, religious, economic, racial—do better than marriages with dissimilarity of backgrounds. This is a matter of percentages. Another fact comes from psychology: A large number of racially mixed marriages are neurotically motivated, and carry within them the seeds of powerful self-punitive and other destructive forces. Still another fact, psychologically and sociologically derived, is that large numbers of individuals in a community, both Negro and white, will reject both partners in a racially mixed marriage. Science, then, is a matter of valid generalizations, and for the counselor generalizations about individual and group behavior, consciously or unconsciously motivated. In a word, it is everything we know about what makes people tick, or tic!

The art of counseling, by contrast, has more to do with when and how to apply what we know about people. An untrained Red Cross junior case aide advised an elderly lady to enter a rest home. She was certain that this was the best solution, but, having advised it, did not press the matter. A day or two later the client announced with evident satisfaction that *she* had decided that the best thing for her to do would be to live in a rest home. The counselor knew that the client must make her own decision. She might have learned this from training and supervision; as it was, she "knew it" from other sources and applied it intuitively.

The art, then, comprises a sense of timing and a sense of tact. It includes also a sense of appropriateness—when the generalizations apply and when they do not. It involves intuitive understanding and empathy, a subjective awareness of what is going on with the other person. It also includes seeing how this particular situation differs from all previous, though similar, ones and how, therefore, to vary one's ways of dealing with it.

It is easy to say that science can be taught and that art cannot. This, however, is an oversimplification. Students can learn the same laws, rules, and techniques and still understand them differently. In this sense, learning itself is partly an art. By the same token, however, tact, empathy, intuitive understanding, and the like can, in some measure, be learned in supervision and improved through experience. "Blind spots" and neurotic inhibitions or other emotional needs can cause us to repeat our mistakes endlessly, but this is not invariable; sometimes we can learn volumes from a few embarrassing blunders. Counselors, if they listen, can learn from clients just as parents can learn from children. This is yet another reason for a modicum of humility in this business!

E. *The Search for Common Ground*

Let us not overstate the diversity of training, settings, goals, and techniques in counseling. Granting the sometimes marked differences in length of professional training and in orientation, there is considerable evidence to suggest that all groups are tending to extend and enrich their professional training and clinical experience. The more this is done, the more the basic training derives from all of the behavioral sciences and becomes uniform. A recent Congress on Mental Health in one of our states was enlivened by a plea for the certification of counselors on the basis of professional training and competence, and the plea was made by a Roman Catholic nun having a graduate degree in clinical psychology.

There are many comparable "straws in the wind." Clinical psychologists, for example, who are, perhaps, in the best position to bridge the gap between the biological and social sciences, nevertheless prefer to treat clients in a clinic or similar setting that offers ready access to medical consultation. Many social workers, particularly those in agencies, have psychiatric consultants, as do clergymen who staff counseling services. The importance of the interdisciplinary team in child guidance and similar clinics has already been mentioned.

Similar tendencies are seen in professional education. Newly established schools of medicine, for example, have teachers of professorial rank from the fields of sociology, psychology, and related fields. One school, not yet open, is expected to have eight professorships in the behavioral sciences. Schools of social work depend less upon psychiatrists and other "outside" teachers than before, but nevertheless put increasing emphasis upon courses in growth and development, personality theory, medical and psychiatric problems, and the like. Reliance upon data from all of the behavioral sciences is increasing, the principal issue being simply that of the most suitable teachers. There is increasing acceptance of the fact that all human behavior, including "problem behavior" is best understood in socio-psycho-biological terms, and that adequate professional training must provide the foundations for this point of view.

F. *Psychoanalysis As a Basic Science*

This book has emphasized the practical aspects of counseling, and one of these—in the author's opinion—is the need to dispel some of the confusion about psychoanalysis. Few counselors employ the *techniques* of psychoanalysis in treating clients. The fact that some counselors do employ free association, dream interpretation, interpretation of transference, and so on does not concern us here; this may

be psychoanalysis, psychoanalytically oriented psychotherapy, or "intensive counseling," depending upon whether
the counselor actually does adhere to the psychoanalytic
model and upon semantics. What is of the highest importance here is the fact that every counselor, whether he
knows it or not, employs theoretical concepts drawn from
psychoanalytic psychology.

Dr. Henry Brosin has recently described psychoanalysis
as "the best basic behavioral science, but not the only one."
He was talking about medical education and of the training
that all physicans need, not just psychiatrists. People not
closely associated with the field often have notions about
psychoanalysis that are dated, or were never true. For example, Freud never advocated complete permissiveness
about sexual or any other matters. His "pan-sexuality" involved a definition of sexual pleasure that encompassed all
bodily pleasure including that, for example, derived from
dancing, swimming, or jumping up and down on an abandoned sofa. He came to consider conflicts related to aggressive or destructive impulses at least as important in human
problems as those connected with sexual or dependency
strivings. He greatly expanded the horizons of personal and
social psychology—normal and abnormal—and thereby made
it possible for psychoanalysis to become a fundamental behavioral science.

Psychoanalysis as a psychology was never systematically
formulated by Freud. He kept adding to his observations
and revising his theoretical formulations, and he felt that
the time for systematic presentation had not yet arrived.
His psychological position has been augmented, defined,
and systematized by such writers as Charles Brenner, Erik
Erikson, David Rapaport, and Robert Waelder. Brenner's
book, *An Elementary Textbook of Psychoanalysis*,[4] is perhaps the best introductory work for a statement of funda-

mental psychoanalytic concepts. It should, however, be supplemented by Waelder's *Basic Theory of Psychoanalysis*[5] and Erikson's *Childhood and Society*[6] for more detailed discussion and application of concepts of ego psychology. Rapaport's *The Structure of Psychoanalytic Theory*[7] is a "must" for those who require a more detailed statement of the scientific validity of psychoanalysis as a comprehensive theory of human behavior.

The practical implications of psychoanalytic psychology for counseling are known to most counselors in some degree, but often incompletely and under other names. One author of a book on counseling, who seems to derive nothing from psychoanalytic sources, nevertheless makes indirect references to transference phenomena and speaks openly of problems operating at an unconscious level. At the same time, however, he is convinced that repression, "in the Freudian sense," does not occur very frequently in the sexual area today. This is so very naïve simply because Freud wrote especially about the repression of *infantile* sexuality —and particularly the young child's *fantasy* life—and relatively little about the uninhibited sexual behavior of adults. In any case, repression is the keystone of the unconscious problems of which this author speaks!

The scope of contemporary psychoanalytic psychology can only be hinted at here. It is empirical in that it rests upon careful observations of human behavior. These observations are as dispassionate as possible. One does not have to like a temper tantrum, for example, or approve of criminal behavior, but one can try to be as objective in observation and understanding as a surgeon removing an inflamed appendix or a pathologist studying cancer tissue under a microscope.

Such observations are made with the working assumptions that all behavior is the expression of the total personality (the organismic point of view) and cannot be isolated (except for descriptive purposes) from the whole person, and also that the behavior of the total individual must be understood in the context of its interaction with its total life situation or environment (the Gestalt, psychosocial, and adaptive points of view). Moreover, any present behavior is partly determined by the developmental experiences of the individual (genetic point of view); by the basic drives (dynamic point of view); by unconscious as well as pre-conscious and conscious determinants, of which the unconscious ones are crucial (the topographical point of view); by psychological energies that regulate but at the same time find expression in behavior (the economic point of view); and by the interaction of psychic structures, the ego, super-ego, and id, among themselves and with the external reality (the structural point of view). All of this encompasses a wide range, but it indicates the theoretical framework that contains our highly important practical awareness of the determining significance of family life, sibling and marital relationships, physical health, neighborhood influences, early identifications, conflicts between home and larger social groups, unconscious motivations, and transference phenomena in counseling.

Another practical aspect of this is the fact, mentioned earlier, that most of us receive only part-training in the behavioral sciences and, particularly, as the preceding paragraph certainly suggests, in the basic science of psychoanalytic psychology. There is at times, moreover, the dangerous tendency to regard the part-training as the essence. For example, therapists who find interpersonal theory easier to comprehend than other aspects of psychic reality (e.g., early fantasies) are likely to take a client's descriptions of his relationships—past and present—at face value. This is, in fact, much easier to do than to evaluate the effects of wish, fear, spite, and expectations of the counselor on the client's story of his life. The counselor is seldom in a position to judge what other people in the client's life are like. He should therefore be very slow to assume the existence of a "rejecting mother" or a "weak, passive father." Even an "alcoholic husband" may turn out to be one who spends one night a week at a tavern. It is well to recall the historian's dictum: A historical fact may be established by the independent testimony of two or more independent witnesses, neither or none of whom is self-deceived.

There appear to be opposing currents of opinion in various professional groups as to what should be taught and as to who should do the teaching. At a time when some medical schools are making greater use of psychologists, social workers, sociologists, and other social scientists as teachers, some schools of social work are striving for professional autonomy and insisting that social work educators must assume responsibility for the social work curriculum. Charlotte Towle has written:

> Perhaps the major reason for the growing trend toward assumption by the social work educator of responsibility for structuring and teaching in this area (personality development) is our desire to solve the problem of the social worker's long-standing overdependence on the psychiatrist. Students, generation after generation, have regarded the psychiatrist as the authority on the whole gamut of human behavior because, with few exceptions, the psychiatrist has been the teacher. If social work educators cannot assume responsibility for this part of the curriculum, we cannot hold our profession responsible to speak and act with the authority of knowledge which should be peculiarly ours. We have had a long and rich experience in deal-

ing with individuals under stress. We should be able
to speak with some authority on normal ego-function-
ing under stress and in many instances to differentiate
the normal from the pathological.[8]

Obviously there are profound reasons for the position
taken by Miss Towle. It is incontrovertible if she is talking
about *external* stress. The fact is, however, that social
workers seldom deal with problems of normal ego-func-
tioning under (external) stress, at least seldom in family and
children's counseling agencies. Both in their theoretical and
clinical training, they are frequently uncertain as to some
phenomena of intrapsychic stress as well as to the evaluation of organic components in total functioning. If there
has been too great dependence on either side in the relationship of psychiatry and social work, then the clients should
go to an analyst (or at least to a marriage counselor) before
seeking a divorce!

It is just as artificial for a social worker to limit himself to
the healthy ego's reactions to stress as it is for a physician
to focus only on the ulcer patient's ulcer. The trend is away
from part-training and from part-applications of training.
Either we all need better, more complete training or we all
need increasingly to collaborate both in teaching and in
practice. If these are not possible, then we must be *highly*
selective—as psychoanalysts are supposed to be—in those
we take for treatment.

The resolution to be highly selective is no real solution,
however. To be selective requires *diagnostic* sophistication.
We cannot resolve to limit ourselves to marriage problems,
for example. For every marital problem that reflects a predominantly current stress, there will be ten that reflect the
individual, but now interacting, problems that the couple
brought to the marriage in the first place. Whatever one's

specialty within the field of counseling or other therapy, there are what doctors call indications and contraindications for therapeutic procedures, and to evaluate these one needs a diagnosis. Once again, then, if we cannot have better training, we must have better collaboration.

The dependence of one helping profession on any other can be replaced by interdependence. Counselors who do not have medical training, for example, do not find it too difficult to work in a medical setting or, at least, to have medical consultation readily available. The physician, clergyman, or lawyer counselor, by the same token, is becoming increasingly aware of the advantages in turning to social workers and psychologists for help. Despite all of the existing vested interests and concerns about status and prestige, the day is almost certainly coming—a day envisioned in the Kennedy proposals for the Mental Health Act of 1963, but tragically thwarted—when community mental health centers will be staffed by representatives of most of the helping professions. In such centers, the diagnostic function may well be more important than the treatment, which can often be carried out elsewhere; the diagnosis, for example, as to whether—in our inadequate present terms—the stress is predominantly organic or emotional, external or intrapsychic. But, better still, an evaluation of the total person in his total situation.

All of the foregoing implies, of course, a "diagnostic orientation" and states that no single professional group has a monopoly on diagnostic methods or diagnostic wisdom. The point is that *theoretical* as much of the above discussion may seem, its *practical consequence* is that no professional group in the field of counseling is in a position to stand alone; that there is greater need than ever before for a pooling of empirical data and an integration of theoretical concepts; and, finally, that all of us need to be as aware of the limitations of our knowledge as we are of its potentialities.

1. James F. Adams, *Problems in Counseling: A Case Study Approach* (New York: The Macmillan Company, 1962), pp. 3–4.

2. Frederick Thorne, "Directive and Eclectic Personality Counseling," in *Six Approaches to Psychotherapy.* (McCary, James L., ed., New York, The Dryden Press, 1955, pp. 235–286.)

3. Maurice Levine, *Psychotherapy in Medical Practice* (New York: The Macmillan Company, 1944).

4. Charles Brenner, *An Elementary Textbook of Psychoanalysis* (New York: International Universities Press, 1955).

5. Robert Waelder, *Basic Theory of Psychoanalysis* (New York: International Universities Press, 1960).

6. Erik Erikson, *Childhood and Society*, 2nd ed. (New York: W. W. Norton and Co., 1963).

7. David Rapaport, *The Structure of Psychoanalytic Theory*, Psychological Issues, Monograph 6 (New York, International Universities Press, 1960).

8. Charlotte Towle, "A Social Work Approach to Courses in Growth and Behavior," *Social Science Review*, 34:404, 1960.

Suggestions for Further Reading

On Personality Development

Blos, Peter, *On Adolescence: A Psychoanalytic Interpretation.*
New York: The Free Press of Glencoe, 1962.

   An authoritative work on the development of the normal
adolescent in our culture. Not concerned with psychopathology or treatment.

Flügel, J. C., *The Psychoanalytic Study of the Family.* Lon-
don: Hogarth Press, 1931.

   An early but still valuable book on child development and
family interaction.

Fraiberg, Selma H., *The Magic Years.* New York: Charles
Scribner's Sons, 1959.

   An unusually lucid account of the emotional and intellectual development of infants and preschool children, indicating particularly the importance of intrapsychic ("magical")
realities.

Pearson, Gerald H. J., *Adolescence and the Conflict of Generations.* New York: W. W. Norton & Co., 1958.

   Designed for students of medicine, psychology, social
work, and others who will engage in counseling, this book,
like that of Blos's, stresses normal development and adaptations to parents and social organization.

Spock, Benjamin, *Common Sense Book of Baby and Child Care.*
New York: Duell, Sloan and Pearce, 1946.

Counselors should read Spock if only to find out what thousands of young mothers rely on. There are several more recent titles. This book gives clear and accurate information about normal development from birth to age seven, including the formation of personality structures.

On Personality Theory

Brenner, Charles, *An Elementary Textbook of Psychoanalysis*, New York: International Universities Press, 1955.

The title might have read: ". . . Psychoanalysis *as Psychology*." The book is a clear and comprehensive statement of psychoanalytic theory for students of medicine, social work, psychology, and related disciplines. There is one chapter on psychopathology; none on treatment.

Engel, George L., *Psychological Development in Health and Disease*. Philadelphia: W. B. Saunders Company, 1962.

Written for medical students, this book will be invaluable to anyone who seeks an integrated statement of psychosociobiological components of health and illness.

Erikson, Erik H., *Childhood and Society*. 2nd ed. New York: W. W. Norton & Co., 1963.

"Required reading" for reasons indicated in Chapter 12.

Freud, Anna, *The Ego and the Mechanisms of Defense*. New York: International Universities Press, 1946.

An exceptionally lucid early formulation of the elements of ego psychology with clinical illustration of important defenses.

Freud, Sigmund, *An Outline of Psychoanalysis*. New York: W.W. Norton & Co., 1949.

Freud deferred writing a systematic account of psychoanalytic theory because he kept revising it. This condensed statement was incomplete when he died, but detailed notes made publication possible. Every word counts!

Gill, Merton M., *Topography and Systems in Psychoanalytic Theory*. Psychological Issues, Monograph 10. New York: International Universities Press, 1963.

By no means an elementary work, this is suggested for those concerned about the scientific validation of psychoanalytic psychology.

Rapaport, David, *The Structure of Psychoanalytic Theory*. Psychological Issues, Monograph 6. New York: International Universities Press, 1960.

The comment about Gill's book applies here, also. This is a definitive statement of the point of view expressed in Chapter 12 about psychoanalysis as a basic science.

Waelder, Robert, *Basic Theory of Psychoanalysis*. New York: International Universities Press, 1960.

This book, like those of Brenner and Erikson, sets forth basic psychoanalytic theory in terms that almost any student of behavioral science or educated layman can understand.

On Psychopathology and Diagnosis

English, O. Spurgeon and Finch, Stuart M., *Introduction to Psychiatry*, 3rd. ed. New York: W. W. Norton & Co., 1964.

Written for medical students, this is a valuable reference for counselors whose training has included lectures on psychiatry.

Menninger, Karl, *The Vital Balance*. New York: The Viking Press, 1963.

Otto Fenichel stated years ago that psychiatric diagnosis is more a matter of dynamisms than of diseases. Menninger extends and expands this point of view. In doing so he also contributes to a unified theory of human behavior in sickness and health. A highly recommended book for counselors of all professions.

Nemiah, John C., *Foundations of Psychopathology*. New York: Oxford University Press, 1961.

Not so much a textbook as the work of English and Finch, this nevertheless gives the essence of psychopathology with many clinical vignettes.

The Encyclopedia of Mental Health. Deutsch, Albert and Fishman, Helen, eds. Six Volumes. New York: Franklin Watts, Inc., 1963.

A complete, authoritative, and invaluable reference work for educated laymen and professionals alike. Its 172 chapters range from Abortion to Young Adulthood. It is highly recommended for all counselors.

On the Theory and Practice of Counseling

Adams, James F., *Problems in Counseling: A Case Study Approach.* New York: The Macmillan Company, 1962.

This book comes from the field of clinical psychology and, together with its helpful references, represents various points of view in psychological counseling.

Bird, Brian, *Talking With Patients.* Philadelphia: J. B. Lippincott Company, 1955.

Written primarily for physicians, this book presents what might be called a medical point of view in counseling. Would that all doctors would read it! Its usefulness is by no means limited to the medical profession, however, and it is recommended for all counselors.

Colby, Kenneth Mark, *A Primer for Psychotherapists.* New York: The Ronald Press Co., 1951.

This book is really addressed to all counselors and is highly recommended.

Ford, Donald H., and Urban, Hugh B., *Systems of Psychotherapy.* New York: John Wiley and Sons, Inc., 1963.

An examination of the theory and practice of prevailing "schools" of psychotherapy.

Hamilton, Gordon, *Theory and Practice of Social Case Work.* 2nd ed. New York: Columbia University Press, 1951.

A standard text for graduate students in social work training, this book has much to offer any counselor. Hamilton is noted for a "no nonsense" approach to the profession and speaks with clarity and authority.

Hollis, Florence, *Casework: A Psychosocial Therapy*. New York: Random House, 1964.

This book is based upon the vast literature of social work supplemented by intensive study of case records in six casework agencies, including a clinic and a hospital. It is a definitive account of the prevailing school of social work counseling by one of its acknowledged leaders. It is very readable, too!

Lippman, Hyman S., *Treatment of the Child in Emotional Conflict*. New York: The Blakiston Division, McGraw-Hill Book Co., 1956.

Since his training with Anna Freud and Aichhorn in Vienna around 1930, Lippman has worked for over thirty years in child guidance clinic settings. He assumes the collaboration of therapists from several disciplines. His title is modest and does scant justice to the wealth of his experience and his material. This is one of the really important books in the field of child therapy.

Nicholds, Elizabeth, *A Primer of Social Casework*. New York: Columbia University Press, 1960.

Social casework is synonymous here with *counseling*. The book is written primarily for social workers who have not had postgraduate training in their profession, but it is addressed also to physicians, clergymen, and teachers. It is highly recommended for all counselors except fully trained social workers who might find it elementary.

Perlman, Helen Harris, *Social Casework: A Problem-Solving Process*. Chicago: The University of Chicago Press, 1957.

Although intended primarily for students in graduate schools of social work and social workers already in practice, the author is so articulate and her writing so lucid that this book can—and should—be read by anyone seriously interested in counseling.

Six Approaches to Psychotherapy. McCary, James L., ed. New York: The Dryden Press, 1955.

Counselors will find several interesting and useful chapters in this book, notably those on client-centered psychotherapy, group psychotherapies, psychotherapy based on psychoanalytic principles, and directive and eclectic personality counseling.

Index